Raymond Gudas

Doberman Pinschers

Second Edition

Everything about Purchase, Care, Nutrition,
Diseases, Breeding, and Behavior, and Training

With 39 Color Photographs

Illustrations by Michele Earle-Bridges

Consulting Editor: Matthew M. Vriends, Ph.D.

BARRON'S

All inquiries should be addressed to:
Barron's Educational Series, Inc.
250 Wireless Boulevard
Hauppauge, NY 11788

International Standard Book No. 0-8120-9015-2

Library of Congress Catalog Card No. 95-19737

Library of Congress Cataloging-in-Publication Data
Gudas, Raymond.
    Doberman pinschers : everything about
  purchase, care, nutrition, diseases, breeding,
  behavior, and training / Raymond Gudas ;
  illustrations by Michele Earle-Bridges.—2nd ed.
      p.   cm.
    Includes index.
    ISBN 0-8120-9015-2
    1. Doberman pinschers. I. Title.
SF429.D6G83   1995   95-19737
636.7′3—dc20

Printed in Hong Kong

6 7 8 9 0   9955   9 8 7

About the Author

Raymond Gudas, former editor of *Pet Age* magazine, has written extensively on animal topics. He is the author of Barron's *Gerbils: A Complete Pet Owner's Manual.*

Photo Credits

Barbara Augello: front cover (Ch Ravenswood Rain Man Aquarius), inside front cover, page 20 (Ch Ravenswood 20 20), inside back cover; Eugene Butenas and Larry Naples (LCA Photography): pages 5, 12, 13, 17, 18, 21 (top left), 37, 54, 55, 59, 85; Susan Green: pages 4, 8, 9, 24, 28, 29, 62, 65, 76; Judith Strom: pages 33, 41, 44, 69, 72; Wim van Vugt: pages 16, 21 (top right, bottom), 50, 80, back cover.

Important Note

This pet owner's guide tells the reader how to buy and care for a Doberman Pinscher. The author and the publisher consider it important to point out that the advice given in the book is meant primarily for normally developed puppies from a good breeder—that is, dogs of excellent physical health and good character.

Anyone who adopts a fully grown dog should be aware that the animal has already formed its basic impressions of human beings. The new owner should watch the animal carefully, including its behavior toward humans, and should meet the previous owner. If the dog comes from a shelter, it may be possible to get some information on the dog's background and peculiarities there. There are dogs that as a result of bad experiences with humans behave in an unnatural manner or may even bite. Only people who have experience with dogs should take in such an animal. Even well-behaved and carefully supervised dogs sometimes do damage to someone else's property or cause accidents. It is therefore in the owner's interest to be adequately insured against such eventualities, and we strongly urge all dog owners to purchase a liability policy that covers their dog.

Contents

Preface

Dogs are routinely described as "man's best friend," but it wasn't always so. Early man and the ancestors of today's dogs were, in fact, rivals. They often competed for the same prey, sometimes even hunting each other in their efforts to survive.

How things have changed! Today, dogs play such an important and varied role in our lives—and in the workings of society at large—that one wonders how we ever managed to get along without them. They serve in the military, help police fight crime, assist the blind and deaf, herd livestock, hunt and retrieve game, draw sleds and carry loads, guard our families and homes, provide companionship, and even make us laugh sometimes with their crazy animal antics.

No one dog can do it all, of course, but when it comes to all-around ability and eagerness to please, probably none comes closer than the stalwart Doberman pinscher. Few breeds, if any, have served man more dutifully or with more enthusiasm. The Doberman is truly a breed apart.

If you have acquired one of these noble creatures, or are contemplating doing so, it is important that you know exactly what to expect, having such a powerful, physically active and generally fearless animal under your charge, and, equally essential, that you understand exactly what is expected of *you* as its master, best friend, teacher, and provider.

The chapters that follow address these and other concerns of the Doberman fancier, and they do so in a way that even the first-time dog owner will find easy to comprehend. The book begins, appropriately enough, with considerations *before* you buy—is the Doberman right for you?; male versus female; puppy versus older dog; and so on. Subsequent chapters deal primarily with the basics of pet care—housing, nutrition, exercise, training, and grooming. Also discussed are the general principles of canine behavior, ailments and injuries, the selection of puppies, and breeding practices.

Utilizing this information will help make your Doberman a better pet and you a better pet owner Certainly that is the intent of all who contributed to this work. This list includes consulting editor Matthew Vriends, Ph.D.; artist Michele Earle-Bridges; Helgard Niewisch, D.V.M., who read the manuscript and made invaluable suggestions; and the talented staff at Barron's, who painstakingly put it all together.

Dr. Vriends and Fredric L. Frye, D.V.M., both provided extensive annotations of the original text, which were incorporated in this new edition.

Raymond Gudas

Finding the right Doberman puppy is a very important task.

Considerations Before You Buy

The Doberman as a Pet

The Doberman pinscher has somewhat of an image problem with the public at large. It is not so much that the common perception of this noble breed is incorrect, but that it is often incomplete and one-sided.

When most people chance upon a Doberman—be it walking obediently at it's owner's side, playing with another dog, or simply resting within the confines of its yard—they may momentarily note its sleekness, grace, and beauty, but the overriding reaction is the sounding of a silent mental alarm, a reminder that, should it mark you as a foe, here is an animal capable of inflicting serious bodily injury.

No doubt it is the common knowledge of the Doberman's role as a police dog, as well as its portrayal in the media (particularly in the fictional landscapes of television and film), that heightens this perception.

As far as potential is concerned, the perception is not exactly unfounded. A strong and fearless animal, the Doberman is more than capable of fending for itself or its master. Should it perceive some person or animal as a threat—rightly or wrongly—the consequences can indeed be severe.

That, however, is only half the story. As most people who own or have owned this breed will tell you, it also makes for a lovable and truly outstanding pet, given certain considerations that pertain to the breed's basic nature.

Behavioral Characteristics

While every dog, like every dog owner, must be evaluated as an individual, the Doberman, like other purebred dogs, has definite behavioral characteristics that are common to the truest representatives of the breed.

Take emotional stability, for example. Despite some arguments to the contrary, the Doberman rates about average in this category when compared with other breeds. While it does not generally display the relative coolness of, say, the Newfoundland, the Labrador retriever, the Siberian husky, or even the Rottweiler (the latter being a part of its genealogy), neither is it as high-strung or temperamental as such dogs as the boxer, the American cocker spaniel, the greyhound, or the Irish setter. Of course, any dog can perform above or below expectations, depending on its breeding, its experience with previous owners (or handlers) and other factors. That's why it's not unheard of to come across an ill-tempered golden retriever or even a sedate Irish setter.

The characteristics in which the typical Doberman excels, and which therefore make it a valued member of the household, are many. Perhaps chief among these is its watchdog/guard dog ability. A Doberman will bark—more than adequately—when confronted by an intruder, sounding the alarm to its master as any good watchdog will do. But it also displays a willingness to take matters into its own hands—

actually, teeth is a better word—and it does so with an eagerness that is generally unrivaled among its working dog counterparts. This is a testimony not only to its self confidence and alertness, but also to its tenacity, all of which tend to be present in generous amounts.

The Doberman also tends to be very territorial, eagerly defending what it perceives to be its own. Not unrelated is the fierce loyalty it displays to family members, this despite the fact that some Dobermans may tolerate the abuses of children better than others, or that some may exhibit a noticeable degree of preference for a particular family member. Such tendencies, however, are by no means unique to the breed. The important thing is that neither behavior be allowed to get out of control.

The Doberman also rates highly in learning ability, which may be considered a measure of its intelligence, and in basic obedience.

Learning ability relates to how fast and to what extent the dog is able to adapt to its social and/or physical environment—in other words, to the fundamental living conditions imposed upon it as an adopted member of your family. This ability includes such factors as the dog's learning response to punishment, as well as its ability to solve problems—opening doors, signaling hunger or the need to go outside, and so forth. Key to these accomplishments is its capacity to retain what it learns and the amount of repetition required before the animal understands what is expected or required of it. In all of these areas, the Doberman scores high marks.

Obedience pertains to social learning, particularly the response to commands. Like many of us, dogs can be underachievers or overachievers in this category. Note also that obedient dogs are not necessarily intelligent dogs, and vice versa. In fact, some dogs

The Doberman's alertness, agility, and sheer physial power are readily apparent to even the casual observer.

credited with above-average intelligence—for example, the Pomeranian, the Chow Chow, the miniature dachshund and the Kerry blue, Lakeland, Scottish, and Welsh terriers—can be rather difficult to train. Fortunately, this is not likely to be an area of great concern to Doberman owners. This dog is a fast and willing learner.

Forceful and vigorous by nature, the Doberman may display a certain intensity in any number of activities, be it reacting to adversity or simply running around during play. Some breeds—for example, the bassett hound, bloodhound, Russian wolfhound, greyhound, saluki and whippet—are active outside, but become relatively inactive indoors; occasionally, as is typically the case with such dogs as Shih Tzu, pug, Japanese Chin, Bichon Friese and French bulldog, the opposite occurs. The Doberman holds a steadier course—very active outdoors, it still exhibits a moderately high activity level inside the home.

Is the Doberman Right for You?

Fairness demands that some considerations be given to the basic nature of

Do you understand the long-term commitment involved in owning a Doberman? A dog should never be purchased impulsively.

you are likely to find your efforts amply rewarded, for you will be entering into a relationship that is sure to bring a great deal of pleasure, love, and security into your life and home.

Selecting a Puppy

Do not be misled by their cute little faces, the plaintive cries of their voices, their clambering to lick you and love you, or their eagerness to play. Buying a puppy is serious business!

Consider yourself fortunate since you've already decided that you want a Doberman. That seems to be half the battle for some people; in reality, it's just the beginning.

Your first course of action should be gathering information and learning as much as possible about the breed. Reading books is the best and easiest way (local libraries, pet shops, and bookstores will help you find what you need), but you will also be well served to attend dog shows, as many as you can if they are held near where you live. Should you find a major show where Doberman pinschers are being displayed, go and observe them in action—in all their glory—for it's here that fine specimens are likely to be found.

The more time you spend studying Dobermans, at shows or elsewhere, the better you'll appreciate true quality when you see it on the street. Or, more importantly, when it's time to select a dog for yourself. But don't stop there. Talk to handlers, breeders, veterinarians, Doberman Pinscher Club and American Kennel Club representatives, and anyone else who is available to answer questions (now's the time to ask) and broaden your knowledge of the breed—or of dogs in general.

Mentioning that you're interested in acquiring a Doberman is often all you'll need to get the conversation started, since many of the people you're likely to meet at shows either are breeders,

the person who desires to purchase a Doberman pinscher as a pet. Simply put, a dominant and energetic dog, which the Doberman certainly is, needs a dominant and energetic owner. Otherwise, both dog and owner are likely to regret the match-up.

While some dogs are naturally submissive, others may try to take over. A very dominant dog may sometimes become difficult when it wants its way, and in some instances may even show some viciousness in getting its "demands" across. It takes an owner with a certain minimum of resolve to keep a bold and capable animal in line.

Similarly, an active, energetic dog needs regular exercise—less if you have a fenced-in yard, more if you don't. It would be unkind and unhealthy to deny a dog like a Doberman the physical activity it naturally craves.

If you are willing and able to accept the special needs and responsibilities that ownership of a Doberman entails, aspire to be, work for one, or can recommend one (or several). Having said that, don't forget that everyone has preferences and prejudices, especially when it involves their own stock, for sale or not.

That's why you should resist any temptation to buy a puppy from the first breeder or salesperson you talk to. No matter how dedicated and knowledgeable he or she may appear to be, no matter how healthy or handsome the puppies for sale may seem, it would be in your best interest to inspect at least a few other litters and to talk to other breeders before making a final decision. After all, the Doberman you choose will likely be part of your life and household for many years to come, so this is not something to be entered into lightly.

Since Dobermans are available in several coat colors (black, red, blue and fawn), it's a good idea to see and get to know them all. And even if you think you know *exactly* what you are looking for, genetics (as influenced by different bloodlines) accounts for more differences, however subtle, than the average person realizes. The more you look around, the better your chances of getting the best dog for *you.*

The Right Choice

That raises an important question: What is the best Doberman for you'? If, like most people, you're simply looking for a good family dog—given that you want a healthy animal and a true representative of the breed—you can find what you're looking for without spending a great deal of money. The purchase price of such a dog should be no more than a few hundred dollars. Top-of-the-line champion stock, on the other hand, will cost many times that.

There is, however, considerable middle ground. For instance, if you have serious plans to enter the show ring or do a limited amount of breeding, or if you simply want (and can afford) to obtain a better-than-average specimen—the result of more selective pairing—you can spend more than the going rate and expect to get a better dog for your money.

With that same thought in mind, if you are committed to the prospect of becoming a full-time breeder, dreaming, perhaps, of producing a dynasty of champions some day, you would be well-advised to acquire a Doberman of genuine aristocratic status—whatever the cost. All things considered, you really do get what you pay for.

That's why it's senseless to look for "bargains" when buying a Doberman, or to make a selection based on price alone. Pricing in the dog-selling business, you will quickly learn, is quite competitive, especially where popular breeds like the Doberman are concerned. In other words, that so-called bargain you have a chance to buy may in the end turn out to be the product of a "puppy mill"—an operation that strives for quantity rather than quality. You might well discover that you have purchased a Doberman that is

Above all, your Doberman puppy must be healthy and possess a temperament typical of the breed.

unhealthy or inferior in some way. Is it worth the risk? Perhaps, if all you're looking for is a basic family dog. After all, a less than "perfect" Doberman can still make a great pet, and even the waifs of this world deserve a chance— but not if you have loftier ambitions.

Likewise, if you spend a small fortune for a show-quality Doberman, but have absolutely no intention of entering it in competition, what is there to be gained? Serious fanciers, in fact, would consider it a sin to deny a potential champion its chance at greatness, at contributing something to the stature of the breed. It's a point not without its merits, when you consider that such an animal is likely to be the result of at least several generations of careful breeding aimed at that very goal.

Where To Start

Whatever your specific intentions, you can start with the local phone book, looking for dog breeders and pet shops that sell Dobermans in the immediate vicinity. You'll also find plenty of nationwide listings in the various dog magazines (*Dog World*, perhaps the best known, is a fine source), but don't overlook the classified ad section of newspapers serving your community. You might get lucky there.

If you'd prefer to play it safe, you can contact the national kennel club for assistance (see page 86). The organization will give you the address of the current Corresponding Secretary of the Doberman Pinscher Club. The Club, in turn, will be happy to furnish you with a list of approved breeders in your area.

Although the odds are very good that you'll be able to find the kind of dog you want within an acceptable distance from your home, do not hesitate to look further if you feel the pickings are slim, or if you are intrigued by the reputation of some of the more prominent breeders located elsewhere.

Transporting animals by air is both safe and reasonably priced, not the nightmare that it used to be. If you don't want to be bothered with the details yourself, there are pet transportation firms that will make all of the necessary arrangements for you; some will even deliver the animal to your door for an additional fee.

How you arrange a long-distance purchase is up to you and the seller. Naturally, it's always best to see and examine the Doberman you are buying for yourself; however, if you can't or don't want to fly (or drive) to the source, but are "sold" on the animal's bloodline and on the integrity of the breeder— and on his or her guarantee of satisfaction—you can complete the transaction via the telephone and the mails.

Note, however, that the success of such a venture hinges a great deal on your clearly and honestly communicating the type of Doberman you want, as well as your long-term goals, if any. All good breeders rely considerably on the reputations they have painstakingly built for themselves, so it really is in their own best interest to make sure that you part company as a happy customer.

Of course, even the best laid plans and the noblest of intentions do not always bring the anticipated results. Not even the breeder, who knows the stock better than anyone else, can promise you that a particular Doberman—especially a puppy—is destined for any specific measure of greatness. Only time will tell and much depends on the nutrition, training and general care the animal receives after it has arrived at its new home.

Buyer Beware

There are, however, certain precautions you can and should take that will at least reduce the risks of your ending up with less of a Doberman than you had hoped for.

First of all, don't even consider a puppy that has not yet been weaned—a process that typically occurs at about six weeks of age. To separate one so young from its mother is cruel and indefensible, and if the pup has not yet been fully introduced to solid foods, it places the animal's health and survival in needless jeopardy. It is also widely believed that removing a puppy from the litter too soon can affect the animal's psychological development, causing problems later on. For these reasons, it's best to wait until the animal is older—eight weeks or more—before removing it from the security of its initial surroundings.

Training only starts between ten and twelve weeks of age, so you needn't feel rushed. As a matter of fact, the longer you wait, the more developed the pup will be, giving you a more complete picture of its physical potential.

Behavior will likewise have developed that much further. Signs of aggressiveness, shyness, and other individual personality traits will be more readily revealed to the patient observer. While extreme shyness or viciousness is undesirable in any pet, it is ultimately a matter of degree. Your choice of personality types may range from a seemingly easygoing Doberman that is more disposed towards obedience, to the kind that tends to be a bit more spirited than might be considered normal. The important thing is that the Doberman fits in with your own personality and life-style.

Male or Female

The sex of the animal accounts for behavioral differences as well. Males do tend to be more assertive than females. As such, they can sometimes be more difficult to house-train, are more likely to fight with other dogs, and are more inclined to roam if the opportunity presents itself. Females, on the other hand, tend to be gentler and more affectionate. For that very reason, they are more often recommended as family dogs—not that there is anything *wrong* with choosing a male puppy instead. It may simply require a little more training and discipline.

If you do choose a female, and at the same time are certain that you will never want to breed or show the animal, it's best that you have it spayed. This will do more than relieve you of the burden of unexpected pregnancy; it will likewise eliminate the twice yearly periods of sexual "heat" when furniture and carpet staining is a concern, at the same time curtailing the annoying antics of lovesick males who might otherwise lay siege to the perimeter of your home. It's also well documented that spaying virtually eliminates the dog's risk of developing breast cancer as it grows older—the best reason of all to have this simple and inexpensive procedure performed.

And if you have ever heard the notion that spaying somehow "defeminizes" a dog, or that a bitch needs to have at least one litter to achieve sexual fulfillment—or any similar such nonsense—forget it. Such assertions are plainly and simply wrong. If anything, spaying is a kindness. Do be certain that you will never want to show the dog, however, as spaying automatically disqualifies an animal from any future competition.

What To Look for

In terms of general behavior patterns, normal, well-adjusted Doberman puppies should be alert, active (but not to the point of being hyperactive), and instinctively curious about what goes on around them. The latter certainly includes the sudden appearance of a new and unfamiliar human face. Your arrival, in fact, should stimulate considerable activity in the litters.

Of course, puppies spend a good deal of time sleeping too; that's to be expected. Similarly, if one or more pups are cautious about approaching you, it doesn't mean that there is something wrong with them. More than likely it's because they simply don't know what to make of you yet. This is especially likely with younger pups who have had little contact with people. Some friendly and reassuring posturing should bring them around.

As far as a Doberman puppy's physical appearance is concerned, there are many clues that reveal its general health and quality. Does the animal appear to be of normal weight? Thinness can be a sign of ill health or nutritional deficiency; obesity, another sign of poor nutrition, could be the result of inferior meat or too high a concentration of fillers in its food.

Diet also plays a part in the look of the animal's coat, which should above all be shiny and clean, and the thicker the better. A dull coat can mean a vitamin deficiency—again suggesting improper diet—and a dirty one deserves comment too, as in the worst case it may suggest a lack of attention by its handlers that could extend to other areas of the animal's care. Inspect the animal's skin by parting hair with your fingers or slowly rubbing your hand against the coat's grain. You should not find parasites, sores, dry scales, or any frequency of insect bites. If you do, buyer beware. It's also a good idea to check the anal area for signs of diarrhea or inflammation.

12

Study the head. Eyes should be clear and free of discharge. A Doberman's lids and rims should be dark. Gums must be pink and even colored, revealing teeth that are bright and clean. Brown stains on teeth indicate that the dog may have had distemper, in which case the stains are permanent. Distemper teeth, as they are called, are not penalized in the show ring, but they nevertheless detract from a dog's good looks. Also inspect the alignment of the teeth. What you're looking for is a true scissors bite, with the lower incisors touching the inside of the upper incisors.

Now's the time to inquire about the animal's diet, about inoculations and any health problems it may have had, and whether the animal has been wormed. While you're at it, ask to see the pedigree—and the sire and dam, if they are on the premises.

Closing the Deal

Most breeders will allow you to have the puppy you select inspected by a veterinarian of your own choice before the sale is officially completed. It's a good idea to take advantage of this opportunity. Even though the veterinarian may not be an expert on Dobermans, he or she will at least be able to size up the animal's general health and its potential for normal development.

The seller of a dog that is eligible for AKC registration is required to provide you with the necessary application form, or at the very least, a written and

Puppies routinely engage in play-fighting with their littermates, instinctively vying for dominance while exploring each other's physical limits.

Humane treatment coupled with proper training fosters the bonds of loyalty that will make your Doberman a valued and trusted member of the family.

ing a trip of longer duration—several hours or more—stop occasionally to offer food and/or water to the animal, especially the latter. Finally, depending on the weather and time of year, make sure your car's heater and air-conditioner are in proper working order. Plan to arrive early in the day, if possible. This will give your pet many hours before nightfall to explore the sights and sounds of its new home. The animal may even get tired enough to sleep through the night without yelping or howling, which puppies recently separated from their litter-mates are likely to do initially.

Dogs and Children

If there are children in your family, it is important that you explain to them—before your Doberman arrives—how to treat the dog properly. They have to learn that it is wrong to bother the animal while it is eating or sleeping, or to pull its ears or tail or otherwise

signed statement including all the information you'll need—the breed, sex, and color of the Doberman; its date of birth; the name of the breeder; and the registered names and numbers of the sire and dam—that will allow you to proceed on your own. If the litter you have inspected has already been registered with the AKC, the assigned litter number is what you'll need. If the seller cannot meet these requirements at the time of sale, you should not proceed with the transaction.

Taking Your Pet Home

If you are transporting your pet to its new home by car, it's best that you do so directly, avoiding the delay of unnecessary stops that prolong what may be a frightening or uncomfortable experience for the animal. Bring a friend or family member with you so that one of you can keep an eye on your Doberman while the other keeps both eyes on the road. If you are fac-

Holding a puppy properly means placing one hand around its chest while supporting its rear end with the other. Never pick up a puppy by the scruff of the neck as this can cause great pain.

mistreat it, even in play. Otherwise, the Doberman may respond by biting, possibly causing serious injury in extreme cases.

The sensible approach is to let children share in looking after the dog, even in such simple ways as changing its water, brushing it (under your supervision), and even taking it for walks (but not before you are sure the youngsters can control the animal). Participation of this kind is sure to foster a friendship between child and dog that's likely to last forever.

Adjusting to Other Pets

Given time, and a little judicious input on your part, a Doberman puppy will usually adjust to other dogs in a household with a minimum of hardship. There are, however, exceptions, and chief among these is the introduction of a second female into a home already occupied by an older female. Adult female Dobermans tend to become possessive of their masters as they grow older, and they may resent the new arrival to the point where some aggression will be displayed. Keep the dogs separated when no one is at home—at least for the first few months—but allow them to come into frequent contact with one another when you are there to supervise them. Eventually, the two should learn to accept—or at least tolerate— each other.

To help achieve this end, it's important that you avoid any hint of favoritism towards either animal.

That means providing separate feeding dishes, separate toys, and separate beds for each one.

More specifically, it means feeding both Dobermans the same food at the same time (comparably smaller amounts for the older dog so it doesn't exceed its normal daily intake of calories); walking them together (so far as this is possible, since puppies will not be able to "go the distance" with an adult dog); and even playing with them together (though not in a way that the animals end up competing for the same toy). Jealousies arise when one of the animals—usually the older dog—sees the other as a rival, or worse, as its replacement. Avoid even the hint of such behavior.

Getting a dog and cat used to each other generally presents problems only if both are fully grown. In this case, there may be an uneasy period of adjustment, but the two should learn to live together in time. Puppies and kittens, on the other hand, typically make friends easily in the course of play.

What About an Older Dog?

It's possible that you may come across a fully grown or even older Doberman that is available for adoption. Should you consider it? If you've had no previous experience with dogs— powerful and domineering ones—the answer is a definite no. Unless you really know what you are doing, you may be asking for trouble. Retraining a fully grown Doberman and gaining its confidence and respect is often a long and arduous process. It requires a level of knowledge and understanding that few novices possess.

The advantage to buying a Doberman puppy is that you start with a clean slate. Not only can you fully enjoy its infancy, watching it develop to adulthood; you also benefit from having a direct and early hand in training the animal and initiating it into your family and life-style. There is much to be said for the bonds of love and loyalty that such an arrangement fosters.

When raised together, Dobermans of the same litter can be expected to establish a bond of friendship that will last throughout their adult lives.

Basics of Care and Management

Perhaps it is simply a manifestation of human nature that people typically buy a dog first, and only then realize that the animal will need a place to sleep, some kind of bowls for food and water, a collar and lead, and various other trappings.

All too often, that means a hasty and incomplete last minute shopping spree, or, if you've purchased your Doberman from a breeder who doesn't happen to carry the supplies you need, an ill-planned stop at the neighborhood pet shop, with the same likely results.

The complaint here does not concern the reckless management of one's time and money, although that argument can be made; above all, it involves the very well-being of the animal itself. New to life, removed from its mother and littermates and from the comfort and security of its birthplace, the young pup has every reason to be apprehensive about its sudden departure into an overwhelming and entirely foreign world.

It's well known that virtually all animals are subject to stress when they undergo a change in environment. For a puppy leaving its "nest" for the first time, the experience can be downright traumatic. In some cases, it can actually lead to health and/or behavioral problems that may be difficult, or at best unpleasant, to correct later on. With precisely that in mind, it is truly in your own and your Doberman's best interest to make preparations for its arrival in advance.

Sleeping Quarters

You should probably start with a bed. The pet industry offers something for every taste and budget. A well-stocked pet store will have at least several types to choose from, ranging from the simplest (and cheapest) floor mats to fanciful basket-type configurations and even genuine small-scale waterbeds complete with heating pads!

Whichever kind you choose, consider one that is large enough to accommodate a Doberman when it is full grown. On the other hand, you might want to start with something more expendable, perhaps even homemade, during the initial house-training phase. That's fine, as long as the bed is kept dry, clean, and comfortable. Although animals instinctively avoid eliminating within their own sleeping quarters, puppies aren't exactly known for neatness—or great body control, for that matter—so you might want to start with shredded newspapers or paper towels as bedding material. Replacement is easy and inexpensive, and you can always switch to better materials—towels, rugs, blankets, or pillows—when the animal has developed self-control.

Placement of the bed is another important consideration. Ideally, it should be out of the way of major foot traffic, but should still be in a position that offers some view of adjoining rooms so the animal doesn't always have to get up to investigate every sound that captures its attention.

Whelping box and sleeping baskets. Make certain you choose one that is large enough for a full-grown Doberman to lie down in comfortably.

Dogs seem to appreciate the luxury of being able to survey their surroundings without having to abandon the warm embrace of a particularly comfortable sleeping position. Consider it a kindness. For obvious reasons, avoid placing the bed near a radiator or other heat source, or in an area subject to drafts. Common sense will dictate that the bed be in a part of the house that is always accessible to the animal when it is inside—not behind a closed door, for instance—or else your pet will find other places to sleep that may not be to your liking (your bed, sofa, favorite chair, or best rug are likely alternatives).

It is important that your Doberman know that it has at least one place in the house that is truly its own. Certainly its sleeping area represents such a place—its own piece of turf, a kind of safety zone where it is secure and, for the most part, beyond interference. That being the case, it is much better to take the time to determine the ideal location for the bed at the outset, rather than changing your mind later on and moving it some-

Whatever type of bed you choose, it should be located in a quiet, draft-free corner of your house.

where else. Doing so may annoy or confuse the animal; it's simply not a good idea.

The Feeding Regimen

The same thing applies to the placement of food and water bowls: find the most convenient out-of-the-way place and try to keep it as a permanent site.

Bowls should be large enough to accommodate a Doberman when it is fully grown. They should also be of sufficient weight and of such design that they will not get overturned or moved around too easily when they are being used. Most bowls are made of metal, clay, or plastic. Clean them regularly, and make sure that a fresh supply of water is always within the animal's reach.

Your newly acquired pet will be facing numerous and rather drastic changes when it first joins your household. It would be wise and kind if diet is not one of them. Before taking the animal home from the seller, find out what it is being fed, including nutritional supplements if any, and on what kind of schedule. Duplicate these as closely as

Food and water bowls are available in all shapes and sizes. Choose bowls that are sturdy and heavy enough to remain stable while an eager Doberman is having its dinner.

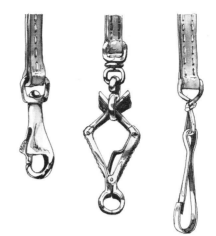

Choke collars (top) are ideal for training your Doberman. Leather collars (bottom left) and nylon collars (bottom right) are also serviceable.

Leashes are available with various types of fasteners: the safety catch (left), the spring clip (center), and the spring catch (right).

possible, at least initially. You can gradually switch to an alternate feeding plan after your Doberman has begun to adjust to its new surroundings.

Collars and Leashes

The collar: Your puppy will need a collar—several, no doubt, before it is fully grown—and a leash to go with it. As far as the former is concerned, you can choose from an almost endless variety, as long as it fits properly, meaning not so tight that it is uncomfortable or annoying, but not so loose that it can get caught on something, perhaps resulting in serious injury. The rule of "thumb" is that you should be able to fit a finger through the collar rather easily as it rests on the dog's neck, but not much more than that.

If you expect the collar to last, a leather one might best be avoided on an active, fully grown Doberman, as it will inevitably come into contact with the animal's body oils, sooner or later creating a terrible odor. Do try to clean the collar with mild soap occasionally, but when it eventually shows the strains of wear, replace it with a new one.

The I.D. tag: Don't neglect one of the prime uses of the collar—that is,

as a place to affix the dog's identification tag. Should you somehow get separated from your Doberman, it will significantly improve your chances of getting it back. It is becoming increasingly commonplace for owners of more valuable dogs to have them tattooed for identification purposes, typically

Leashes come in all shapes and sizes, and some are rather fanciful. For instance, the type incorporating a reel mechanism (above) allows the handler to increase its length at the press of a button.

Genetics, as influenced by different bloodlines, accounts for more differences, however subtle, than the average person realizes. The more time you spend studying Dobermans, at dog shows or elsewhere, the better you'll be able to judge true quality when you're ready to select one for yourself.

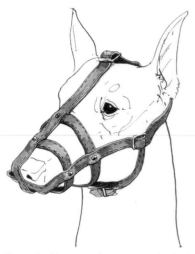

If you decide to purchase a muzzle, look for one that can be adjusted in size as the dog grows.

regularly—a little every day or at longer, designated sessions during the week (see page 25). A brush with hard bristles works best. For dealing with the inevitable parasites, it is also recommended that you acquire a flea comb, flea powder or spray (only brands that are specifically designated for use on dogs), and tweezers (for ticks, primarily).

Toys

Finally, we come to the subject of "toys," a bit of a misnomer since all of these items—beef or nylon bones, rawhide chews, rubber balls, and so on—do more than simply entertain or amuse the animal. In addition to remedying boredom, they also facilitate exercise to varying degrees, and in the case of bones and chews, contribute to healthy teeth and gums as well.

Buy only those playthings with labels specifying that they are made for dogs. There are scores of such items to choose from, and this is the only way to ensure that your pet will not be exposed to toxic or otherwise dangerous materials, such as plastics that can splinter or metal parts that

around the groin area or the inside of the ear. It is a painless and inexpensive procedure, it is accepted in the show ring, and it has had very good results, both in curbing thefts and in finding lost dogs' owners. Animal control authorities routinely check recovered dogs for tattoos, so if your pet should fall into their hands, they'll find you. If you do opt for a tattoo, don't forgo the tag on the collar—it's simply that much more insurance that you won't lose a friend.

The leash: The main consideration in choosing a leash for your pet is its length, which should be a comfortable one for both you and the animal. There is, however, an additional consideration where a puppy is concerned—namely, that the leash not have any exposed chain or metal parts. Given the chance, a puppy is likely to chew its leash, and the metal can damage its teeth.

Grooming Supplies

To help keep the animal's coat looking its best, you should brush it

A toy must never be so small that it may be swallowed by your dog, and it should always be made of materials that are not harmful to the animal.

can harm teeth or be swallowed, perhaps with tragic results.

My tip: Resist any urge you may have to give your dog old shoes, towels, or articles of clothing to play with. Doing so may send the wrong signal to the animal, and you may come home someday to find that your pet has been foraging for new playthings in your clothes closet!

Your Dog's Home

If you live in a house with a yard, you have the option of letting your dog live outside—that is, in a doghouse. Most Dobermans adapt quite well to such a life-style.

You're likely to be surprised at the number and variety of doghouses that are available today, though no single pet store can be expected to carry more than a few models of any one size. Shop around. This is an important investment if it's going to be the animal's permanent home.

The most important requirements are that the design features allow for proper ventilation in hot weather and the retaining of body heat during winter months, and that the shelter be large enough—which means that your Doberman should be able to

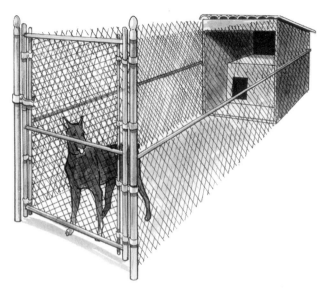

An outdoor run should be attached to a shelter that is durable enough to protect the dog against rain, direct sunlight and cold temperatures.

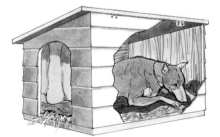

Among the features of a first-rate doghouse are a hinged top for easy cleaning, appropriate bedding material covered with a soft blanket, and a doorway that is just large enough for the animal to pass through. (In cold weather, the opening should be covered to keep body heat inside.)

stand upright or lay fully outstretched inside it.

Other commendable features of a doghouse include the following: a durable surface; adequate insulation; a roof that is slightly extended for extra shade, slanted for improved circulation of air, and hinged or removable for easy cleaning; a slightly raised lip at the foot of the doorway to keep bedding in place; and perhaps even an extended front "deck" so your pet can lay at least partially outside when the weather is nice.

As far as your own input as a dog owner is concerned, the shelter must be kept clean and dry as a first line of defense against germs and parasites. That means cleaning it periodically (with hot water and a mild disinfectant) and changing the bedding whenever it's necessary. Cedar shavings, available in any pet store, are perhaps the best bedding material because they are soft and highly absorbent, and because they have a deodorizing effect. An alternative is using straw as a floor dressing with a blanket placed on top of it.

Ideally, the shelter should be placed in a location that is neither completely exposed to the constant rays of the sun, nor swallowed in permanent shade. It's also recommended that you raise the structure off the ground slightly to guard against damage from moisture.

Since your Doberman will be spending most of its time in the yard, you should carefully inspect the perimeter to satisfy yourself that it is escape proof, be it by jumping, digging, or climbing. As an additional precaution, it would be wise to place a "Beware of Dog" sign (or one of its more expressive equivalents) on every gate to give errant neighbors and other innocents fair warning of the animal's presence. Actually, you may even want to consider buying locks for the gates, both to prevent accidental incursions into

your yard and, however unlikely in a Doberman's case, to provide an extra safeguard against "dognapping." In a more probable scenario, it would eliminate the possibility of someone accidentally or deliberately leaving the gate unlatched. Unfortunately, that's the kind of opportunity that many dogs, however loyal, can't resist.

If you are handy and decide that you want to build a doghouse yourself, follow the previous recommendations for the best results. Remember to stick to hardwoods and to use only nontoxic (lead-free) paint. The novice builder may be better off obtaining a blueprint design from the Humane Society, which distributes them free of charge, or from the local library. Modify the plans if you wish, but at least they'll provide a solid point of reference.

Even if your Doberman will live outdoors most of the time, there will be occasions—if the animal is ill, or if the temperature drops below freezing—when it should spend the night inside with you. That probably means you'll need another bed, as well as a suitable location for it. Take care of these details at the outset.

If yours will be primarily an indoor dog and you don't have a fully contained yard to let it romp during periods of the day (or if you have a large yard but don't want the animal to have access to all of it), you still have several options. You can build a run—that is, a separate fenced-off enclosure (the bigger the better) where the dog can safely be left to its own devices for intervals of an hour or two; or you can opt for the much less expensive solution of a tie-in stake. There are several brands on the market. Securely anchored into the ground, they will confine your Doberman within a circumference determined by the length of its leash. This method, also, should not be employed for longer than an hour or two at a time.

These self-assured young Dobermans have great energy and vivacity!

Grooming

Like other short-haired dogs, the Doberman pinscher does not require a lot of grooming, but regular attention—not only to the coat, but also to nails, teeth, and ears—is still necessary to keep the animal looking and feeling its best.

The Basics of Brushing

Brushing the dog regularly (if not every day, at least twice a week for ten minutes or so each session) will help keep both coat and skin healthy. Besides loosening dandruff and stimulating blood circulation, it also removes loose hair that may be trapped within, at the same time distributing the skin oils that make the coat shine. You've got to admit, that's a pretty decent return for such a small investment in time.

No doubt the most practical motivation for brushing your pet regularly is to remove the loose hairs that will otherwise end up all over the house. Animals in the wild—and dogs that live outdoors most of the time—generally shed once a year, during the spring months. Dogs that spend most of their lives indoors, however, are less predictable in their shedding patterns; some may even shed constantly, owing to the relatively constant warm temperature in the home, as well as frequent exposure to artificial light. Brushing will help keep the situation under control.

For the Doberman, a moderately stiff brush, available at any pet store, will do the job nicely. Use it gently, but go all the way down to the skin, brushing in the direction of the coat. Use a comb to work out the occasional mat; for tougher jobs—like paint, tree sap, tar, and similar substances—soak the area with mineral or vegetable oil for 24 hours, then try washing it with soap and water. It's best *not* to use kerosene, turpentine, or the like on your pet, as these can be harmful to the animal.

Bathing

Like it or not, there will be times when your Doberman needs a bath. You won't need a calendar to figure out the frequency; your nose will tell you. Some pet owners use their own bathtubs to wash their dogs, and there's really nothing wrong with it, since you can clean the tub afterwards. Other people find the idea distasteful, and perhaps that's understandable too.

Unless you are prepared to install a special tub for your pet (perhaps in your basement, if you have one), or have access to a freshwater lake, you have two basic alternatives—wash the dog outside, assuming the weather is agreeable, or have a professional groomer do it for you.

The advantages of seeking the services of a professional are many. Not only can you expect to get a thorough, first-rate job at reasonable cost, but you can also benefit immensely from his or her knowledge and experience. For example, groomers are often the first to notice that a dog has an ear infection, skin disorder, or other ailments that require a veterinarian's care, and of course, they are your best source for recommendations

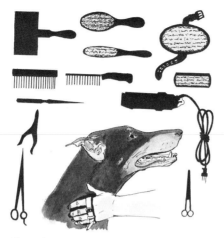

If you have your pet groomed professionally with some frequency, you probably won't need the full complement of grooming tools that are available. Nevertheless, you will still need a moderately stiff brush to use at home, as well as a comb to work out the occasional mat.

Be careful not to get irritating substances in your pet's eyes. Prolonged exposure will cause an infection. Symptoms include redness and/or a discharge from the eye. For mild irritations, you can wash the eye with any of several special preparations available at pet stores—follow directions! For more serious irritations, you'll have to seek professional help from a vet.

If you are working indoors, you'll want to "squeeze" excess water from the coat immediately after rinsing, and be prepared to toss a towel over the animal before it can execute its traditional water-removing shake. Leave your Doberman indoors until its coat dries completely (even if you have washed it outside), both as a health precaution and as insurance that the animal won't get into something again while its coat is still wet.

If your pet should ever have an encounter with a skunk (which isn't as unlikely as you may think, considering that the malodorous mammal is found throughout North America and that dogs have a penchant for terrorizing small animals), the only proven remedy is soap and water. Wash the dog—twice if necessary and let time (and fresh air) take its course. In a day or two, the experience will be nothing more than a bad memory. Rumor has it that rinsing with tomato juice helps neutralize the smell. Diluted lemon juice is also frequently recommended.

My tip: There may be occasions when you detect a particularly foul odor around the dog's neck area. This could be the result of an ear infection, in which case a veterinarian's care is called for, or it could simply mean that it's time to clean or replace the animal's collar. Besides oil glands that keep the coat shiny and water-resistant, a dog's skin tissue also contains so-called sebaceous glands, which secrete sebum, a fatty substance that coats the hair shaft as it grows. Sebum often

involving grooming maintenance at home—all that, and you haven't gotten your hands wet.

If you do decide to bathe the dog yourself, just be sure that you buy a shampoo that is labeled as being specifically formulated for dogs. Human shampoos—even so-called "baby" formulas—are best avoided, as they tend to dry out the animal's coat and skin too much. Dog shampoos are also preferable because they usually contain flea-killing agents, a wise safeguard against potential infestation.

Whichever system you choose, the procedure is essentially the same: wet the Doberman's coat (with water neither too hot nor too cold), work in the shampoo, and rinse thoroughly. Always read the label for product warnings or special instructions, such as how long the shampoo should remain in the dog's coat for its pesticide to be effective.

collects and becomes trapped underneath the collar, creating an aroma that will not go unnoticed for long.

Cleaning the Ears

Your dog's ears will require some attention as well. Clean them every month or so using a damp cloth or towel soaked in mineral oil. Do not probe into the ear canal, as this can result in injury. If you notice a heavy accumulation of wax inside the canal, it's best to let your veterinarian handle the situation. Slight accumulations can be cleared with an otic solution, which you can obtain from your veterinarian.

If you notice your Doberman shaking its head violently or pawing at its ears, it could mean that it has acquired an infection of some kind. Do not attempt to treat the problem yourself. Take your pet to a veterinarian at the first opportunity.

Some Dobermans have excessive hair growth in the ear canal, and this condition may contribute to infections. If so, your veterinarian may recommend that some of the hairs be plucked to improve air circulation. You can even do it yourself: Using tweezers, carefully remove only those hair shafts that come out with minimum effort.

The Anal Sacs

Another potential grooming concern involves the fluid-bearing anal sacs, whose pungent contents are used to mark territory. Typically, the substance is released during normal defecation, but it may be discharged when the animal is frightened or involved in a fight.

Sometimes the anal sacs become clogged, causing the glands to become enlarged. To prevent infection, they must be emptied. You can have your veterinarian (or even your groomer) do this for you, but you may as well witness the procedure so you can learn how to do it yourself. It's a fairly simple task, despite its unpleasantness, but it requires a certain amount of precision to minimize discomfort to the animal.

If you fail to notice the initial swelling of these glands during routine inspections of your pet, you'll know something's wrong from signals the animal will give you. Typically, it will drag its rear end on the ground in an attempt to alleviate the condition, and it will also resort to frequent licking of the troubled area. At that stage, it may be best to have your veterinarian correct the problem.

It goes without saying that the best time to introduce the grooming regimen is when your Doberman is still a puppy. The animal is more impressionable at a young age, and is therefore more likely to succumb to your preening and probing. Many dogs actually seem to enjoy these regular sessions of attention from their masters, but there are those that, for whatever reason, simply do not take kindly to being handled with such familiarity. Be gentle but firm—your Doberman must (and will) learn to tolerate your actions, for they are necessary for the animal's own good.

After cleaning and brushing you may use a chamois cloth for the finishing touches.

Electric clippers can make parts of the grooming much easier.

Regular, gentle cleaning of the ears is essential.

After clipping the nails, a small electric grinder may be used to trim sharp or ragged edges.

29

HOW-TO:
Caring for Nails and Teeth

Many pet owners who are extremely conscientious about their Doberman's coat, pay little attention to its teeth and nails. This is a grave mistake. Proper care of teeth and nails plays an important role in your pet's health and comfort.

Nail-trimming

Unless your Doberman spends a lot of time walking (or running) on concrete or other hard surfaces, you'll need to trim its nails as often as every two or three months. Some people feel a little squeamish about doing this themselves, but it's really quite a simple procedure—and painless for the animal. Of course, you must have the right tools (a special nail clipper for dogs and a small file, available

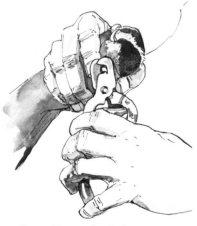

Several types of nail clippers are available. The guillotine type, illustrated above, performs the job well.

at any pet store) and know how to use them properly.

What you want to trim off is the "hook," the part of the nail that turns downward. If you trim any higher, you risk cutting into the "quick," the vein that runs through most of the nail—and which can bleed rather profusely when severed. The quick is visible to the naked eye on most light-colored dogs; with dogs whose nails are black, like the Doberman, you can often spot the area by illuminating the nail with the beam of a flashlight.

Accidents do happen occasionally, and it's not unlikely that you may clip one of the nails too high some day. Don't panic, for it's not a major incident. Apply styptic powder to the wound (don't wait for an accident before you buy some), and the bleeding will stop.

If the above scenario really does bother you, consider filing the nails down instead. Shorten them at least to the extent that they don't touch the floor when the animal walks. Of course, you also have the option of having a groomer do the job for a nominal charge, or even your veterinarian—if you see it needs doing while you are in for a visit.

Why bother clipping nails in the first place? Because not doing so can deform your Doberman's feet, permanently affecting its stance. There's also the chance that a long nail can snag on something and break off entirely. The animal will recover from such an injury, but it will suffer needless pain—and only because of your inattentiveness.

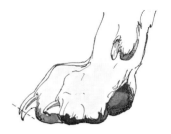

Clip your Doberman's nails at an angle, making sure that you do not cut into the quick.

My tip: Inspect your pet's nails regularly, and if you really want to stay ahead of the game, take it for a lot of long walks—it'll do both of you good.

Dental Care

It's also important that you regularly inspect your Doberman's teeth. Does the animal have bad breath? That usually signals that there is a gum problem of some kind.

Gum problems are more common in older dogs, but pets as young as nine months of age have been known to require professional teeth cleaning because deposits of calculus and tartar had formed on their teeth and gums.

Calculus is a stone-like material that accumulates on teeth, acting like a splinter under the gums. Infection often follows, eventually leading to bone and tooth loss. Frequently, this occurs without any noticeable abscesses in the dog's mouth. The only symptoms may be

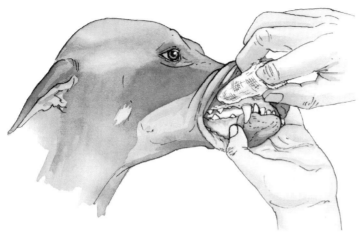

Use a soft toothbrush or a damp cloth to remove superficial debris and plaque from your Doberman's teeth.

bad breath and/or red or bleeding gums.

Yellow stains on the teeth may be caused by plaque, which is constantly forming on the tooth surface. Soft, sticky foods are said to contribute to plaque formation, just as hard foods, kibble, biscuits, bones, and the like—help scrape some of it off. Plaque will form regardless of diet, however, eventually calcifying and turning into calculus. At the back of the mouth, on the cheek side of the molars, is where calculus build up is the greatest.

To deal with the problem, veterinarians recommend routine cleaning of dogs' teeth with a thin washcloth or piece of gauze. Wrap the material around your index finger and use it like a toothbrush, rubbing teeth and gums with a back-and-forth or circular motion.

If your pet needs coaxing, you can try rubbing beef- or chicken-flavored bouillon powder on your makeshift toothbrush. Believe it or not, there's even a beef-flavored toothpaste formulated specifically

for dogs, though it really isn't necessary to use paste or powder of any kind, since light friction is the most important aspect of the cleaning process. (*Never* use "human" toothpaste on a dog's teeth, as its detergents are too strong for an animal's digestive system.)

However you choose to proceed, start when your Doberman is still a puppy and be careful not to upset or frighten it when introducing this new routine. If you upset your puppy, it may forever resist you in all future attempts. Keep sessions brief, and be sure to reward its cooperation with plenty of petting and praise.

Some people use a regular toothbrush on their pets' teeth. If you want to try one on your dog, make sure it is soft-textured, and apply the same technique as in the previous example—that is, short sessions with lots of praise (and a little flavoring, if it helps).

Regular removal of plaque—at least several times a week—can prevent serious gum disease later on. An additional benefit is that it reduces the frequency of professional cleaning by a veterinarian.

Nutrition and Exercise

Your Doberman's overall well-being will largely be determined by both the quantity and the quality of the food you will provide it. Simply put, whether your pet will be healthy or sickly, irritable or happy, well behaved or mischievous, will depend to a great extent on its regular daily diet.

Surprisingly, many pet owners seem unaware of this simple fact—a pity, for an improper diet is the source of a great many problems that can otherwise be avoided. Degenerative conditions attributable to nutritional imbalances include obesity, arthritis, chronic gastrointestinal ailments, and a variety of skin disorders. Those that do not progress to the stage where they actually reduce your dog's life span will at the very least deplete the animal's spirit and energy, compromising its ultimate value as a pet.

A Doberman that enjoys a well-balanced diet, on the other hand, is more likely to achieve—and maintain—its full genetic potential. It will probably benefit from increased stamina, a more positive mental disposition, and even an improved appearance, both in anatomical terms and, most noticeably, in the condition of its coat. The latter, of course, is the most obvious indicator of a dog's general state of health: a shiny, thick coat is a sign of nutritional vitality; a dull, uneven one is your first clue that something may be wrong.

The Function of Nutrients

Before making an intelligent decision as to what to feed your Doberman, it is helpful to understand the basic function of nutrients, the chemical components needed for optimal growth, body maintenance, physical energy, and reproduction—all of which result from complex metabolic reactions within the body.

Nutrition to fuel these reactions is delivered in the form of proteins, carbohydrates, fats, vitamins, and minerals. Protein contains an assortment of amino acids, the basic structural components, while carbohydrates and fats provide energy. Minerals and vitamins are essential because they regulate the body's metabolism.

Protein

The most practical and useful source of high-quality protein for dogs is found in meat. Unfortunately, meat quality can vary a great deal. A major consideration in the development of a feeding program, therefore, should be the quality and ease of assimilation of the protein it provides. That's important because many of the essential amino acids available in meats cannot be synthesized by dogs. For that reason, each day's intake is crucial. If there is a deficiency in one or more of these amino acids, the animal's body will automatically distribute those available to the most vital life functions first, depriving skin, coat and bones of proper nutrition.

Carbohydrates

A similar set of circumstances applies to carbohydrates. While being a vital source of energy, in their raw form they cannot be fully assimilated by dogs. Animals in the wild circumvent this problem because they consume predigested carbohydrates from the stomachs of their prey. When processed in the manufacturing of dog food, these compounds must be converted to a comparable form. If raw or improperly cooked, they can actually undermine a good feeding program, having a tendency to ferment in the animal's intestines. The source and preparation of carbohydrates are therefore the most important factors in their digestibility. It is important that fiber—a complex chemical form of carbohydrates—be available as well. Such roughage allows for optimum digestion; it also promotes controlled elimination of the lowest volume.

Fats

With an energy concentration more than twice that of protein or carbohydrates, fats are crucial in providing energy to fuel body processes. They also supply essential fatty acids that are necessary for daily health. Of all the available animal sources, pure high-quality lard and poultry fat are best because they have a lower melting point than other forms, which means they are more easily absorbed. An additional advantage is that they are better-tasting.

Vitamins

Vitamins encompass a variety of organic substances found in different kinds of foods. Their main function is as components of (and catalysts for) the body's enzyme systems. They also maintain a balance between constructive and destructive cell changes, helping dogs resist disease and infection.

Vitamin A, for example, is necessary for dim-light vision, to maintain healthy skin, and for proper growth. Vitamin D is involved in bone formation, reproduction, and the absorption of minerals from the intestines. Vitamins B_1 and B_6 affect the nervous system, cir-

culation and the gastrointestinal tract; B_2 affects the condition of the skin; B_{12} is involved in the maturation of red blood cells; C helps maintain bone joints, gums and teeth; E is important in reproduction and normal muscle development; K influences the blood's clotting ability.

Minerals

There are at least 14 minerals essential for life, and these have several functions in a dog's body. Elements of teeth and bone, they also regulate body fluids and, like vitamins, serve as catalysts for the body's chemical reactions. Calcium and phosphorous, together with Vitamin D, are vital in tooth and bone development; magnesium is prominent in the latter cause as well; sodium, potassium, and chloride control the fluids involved in perspiration, elimination of body waste, and respiration; iron is essential in the formation of hemoglobin, which distributes oxygen through the bloodstream; iodine stimulates the thyroid gland, which regulates the rate of

Put puppy's dish in a quiet corner, preferably in the kitchen, where the floor can be washed.

33

metabolism; cobalt helps produce Vitamin B$_{12}$.

These trace minerals, like many nutrients, are only required in small quantities. Excesses and imbalances can actually be dangerous to your pet. Moreover, in creating a balanced diet, it's not enough that all the nutrients are there; it's the proportion and order of those nutrients in the food that is more critical.

As you might imagine, if dog owners had to rely on their own wits to provide a balanced feeding program for their pets, it is unlikely that the animals would fare nearly as well as they do. Instead, of course, the vast majority of people depend on commercial manufacturers to feed their pets. Unfortunately, supplying commercial dog food does not guarantee that all of your dog's nutritional requirements will be met.

Why not take advantage of scientific progress as well as convenience? The majority of commercial dog foods contain all the elements a dog needs in the proper proportions.

Commercial Dog Food

It's bad enough that consumer preference in choosing dog food is more likely to be determined by price or packaging than on what it offers an animal nutritionally. What makes the situation worse is the fact that some commercial dog foods are so nutritionally bankrupt that utilizing them in a steady diet is an invitation to serious health problems. Many that claim to be nutritionally complete for example, contain vitamins, minerals and other nutrients that never nourish the dog because its system cannot digest them. Either the manufacturer is ignorant of nutritional needs or is more concerned about making a buck than delivering honest goods.

It is not the purpose of this book to recommend a particular brand of dog food for your Doberman. Besides, there are many high-quality foods manufactured commercially that would do justice to almost any dog's feeding program. Nevertheless, you aren't likely to go wrong if you buy one of the premium brands available in most pet shops, even if management has a vested interest in promoting one particular brand over another, as is sometimes the case. Most are high caliber, nutritionally balanced diets representing the best knowledge we have about animal nutrition. You may, however, want to visit several shops and inspect the sales literature of different brands before finally making your selection.

Supermarket brands require a bit more judgment. While generally not as sophisticated as the specialty brands found in pet stores, many—especially the well-known national brands—do provide the minimal daily nutritional requirements to keep an animal in decent health. The foods to avoid without question are the obscure, so-called "bargain" brands, which are more likely to contain inferior and even harmful ingredients.

That is why the majority of veterinarians also advise against using generic-type pet foods. Many are produced with little or no analysis, resulting in nutritional deficiencies that can contribute to skin and coat problems and even to digestive and intestinal disorders.

Shortcomings of "Bargain" Brand Foods

There is, in fact, solid clinical proof that there is a nutritional difference between dog foods that claim to be "complete and balanced" and that "bargain" and generic brands fall considerably short of national and pet store brands. A recent study of "bargain" brand foods undertaken revealed shortcomings in basic palatability as well as in digestibility of nutrients. Of 78 brands tested, 65 (or 83 percent) failed to meet National Research Council Standards for seven critical nutrients analyzed. What's more, half of them failed to meet their own guaranteed label analysis!

High quality dry, semi-moist, and canned dog foods are available at most pet shops.

Another study, this one conducted by the University of Georgia College of Veterinary Medicine, had even more conclusive results. Researchers divided 21 puppies from three litters into four feeding groups, each with roughly the same number of males and females at similar weights. A single control group was put on a diet of a major, nationally distributed dog food, while the other groups were fed one of three "bargain" brands, each claiming to be nutritionally complete for a growing puppy. After ten weeks, researchers assessed their findings.

Pups fed the national brand gained an average of 21.05 pounds (9.55 kg) during the test, while those given the "bargain" diet gained only 16.4 pounds (7.44 kg). Similarly, puppies fed the better quality food grew an average 7.2 inches (18.3 cm) in body length, while their undernourished counterparts grew just 5.95 inches (15.1 cm). Looked at another way, it was determined that the dogs required 4.45

pounds (2.02 kg) of the national brand for each pound of weight gained: the figure for the "bargain" brands was 5.9 pounds (2.68 kg), which means that, even though "bargain" brands cost less, larger amounts are required to provide the same amount of nutrition as the national brand.

Researchers also noticed that the dark coats of the puppies being fed the low-cost brands were starting to turn gray by the end of the test. When it was over, these animals were put on a better diet, and all gradually returned to normal size and body condition. The tests left no doubt that the biggest distinction between "bargain" brands and their more expensive competitors isn't price at all—it's nutrition. Put simply, one gets what one pays for.

Types of Commercial Dog Food

There are four basic types of dog food—canned, dry, semi-dry, and semi-moist.

Canned food typically contains all the necessary nutrients a dog needs. It consists of some combination of meats (muscle, heart, liver, lung, and so forth), grains (rice, barley, oats, wheat, corn) and added vitamins and minerals.

Dry and semi-dry food has (or should have) basically the same composition, except that moisture content has been reduced or eliminated during the manufacturing process. A dog eating these types of foods makes up for the loss of moisture by simply drinking more water.

Semi-moist food is likewise nutritionally complete if, as in all cases, it is prepared by a reputable manufacturer. The difference is that its moisture content lies somewhere between that of dry and canned food, which means that the dog's need for fluids is, again, only partially satisfied. As with dry and semi-dry food, sufficient amounts of water must be provided to supply the rest.

Rawhide articles are good for your Doberman. Besides providing some benefit in tartar removal, they also give a teething puppy or a bored adult something to play with.

A Healthy Diet

You can still give your Doberman meat, eggs, cottage cheese, and other fresh foods to supplement its regular diet, but if you use one of the many fine-quality commercial foods available today, it is not a necessity as far as health is concerned. Your best reason for varying diet will simply be to provide your pet with a welcomed change of menu. After all, no one likes to eat the same food day after day. The same applies to canned food. Assuming, again, that the brands you use are of good quality, it is nevertheless recommended that you regularly switch "flavors" (chicken, liver, beef, and so forth) to maintain variety in your feeding program.

This is a fairly simple undertaking when you consider the tremendous variety of dog foods in the marketplace. You can, in fact, find a commercially prepared food geared to every age bracket of your Doberman's life, from puppyhood to old age, with various additions and modifications directed towards special health needs. What's more, contents and nutrients are clearly listed on the labels, as are feeding instructions based on the dog's age, size, and weight. Let these, and your conscience, be your guide.

How often you feed your pet is up to you, with several important qualifications. Until they are twelve weeks old, for instance, puppies should be fed four times a day—they need the extra nourishment to fuel their growth. Likewise, from three to six months of age, a program of three meals a day is ideal. After six months, two meals a day are enough, at least until the animal is one year old, when you can switch to a once-a-day feeding schedule if that is most convenient for you.

Many pet owners prefer to remain on a twice-a-day schedule, thus dividing their animals' daily food intake into two halves. Their position is that it is better for the dog's digestion and that it ultimately seems more satisfying—both to the pet owner and the dog. Certainly it offers a better chance of keeping the dog from hanging around the dinner table every night. Pet owners who prefer a once-a-day program can minimize such hassles by giving their dogs a few biscuits, or some other kind of treat, to chew on.

Whichever dietary regimen you eventually adopt, the most important consideration is that you do not overfeed your pet. Follow feeding instructions to the letter, and be mindful of your Doberman's general appearance. If the dog seems to be gaining weight, reduce its food intake or switch to a fitness-type food; if it seems to be getting thin, increase the amount of food you give it.

Note that pregnant or lactating bitches, hardworking dogs, and those that spend a lot of time outdoors in cold weather will require greater amounts of food than the norm prescribes. Remember also that dogs, like people, are individuals. Two Dobermans of the same size and activity range might very well need different amounts of food simply because of varying metabolisms.

The Digestive Process

In the area of digestion, dogs are very different from humans. We grind our food into small particles that are mixed with amylose (a digestive enzyme) before it is swallowed. Dogs tend to swallow food in big gulps. For them, the digestive process does not actually begin until food reaches the stomach.

After passing down the esophagus to the stomach, muscle contractions mix the food with gastric juice, a combination of saliva and other secretions stimulated by contact with the stomach lining. The gastric juices contain enzymes and acids. These substances curdle milk, soften albumen, and help break down fibers and tissues.

The process of breaking down food is called denaturing. When completed, the food is changed into a thick liquid known as chyme, and in this form passes into the small intestine. Once there, other digestive fluids, including those from the pancreas and from the walls of the small intestine, join with liver bile stored in the gallbladder and mix with the food. From here, a number of highly specific enzymes are passed into the intestines.

The two major protein-digestive enzymes, chymotrypsin and trypsin, break down proteins into peptides and single amino acids, while others change starches into saccharides and simple sugars, or split fats into fatty acids and glycerines. As the food is broken down, it travels via the blood system to the liver, the major organ in the body for protein-building. It is during this process that the amino-acid composition of the digested protein becomes critical.

Food that is high in animal or meat protein will come closest to supplying all of the body's requirements for protein-building. A diet that is high in soy or corn, however, may not provide adequate levels of essential amino acid to do the job.

After food substances are circulated by the blood and are either utilized or stored by various cells, waste materials must be eliminated. The kidney, via the urinary system, excretes some metabolic waste products from the inner cells of the body. Most indigestible materials, plus remaining waste, pass into the large intestine and are eliminated.

A good diet and plenty of exercise will keep your Doberman in fine physical condition.

The Importance of Exercise

A nutritionally complete diet is a great foundation for health, but it won't keep your pet's muscles toned, or even free of fat. If you want to keep a Doberman in top physical condition, you'll have to make sure that it gets plenty of exercise.

Most dogs need about an hour of physical activity each day to keep them fit. At least part of that time should be spent running, preferably off the leash—obviously under constant supervision. The easiest way to do this is to take the animal to a large open field and have it retrieve a ball or stick or other suitable object. (Frisbees are great fun, as they allow an interesting range of throwing maneuvers.)

Alternatives include swimming, hurdle jumping—even jogging, should you or another family member engage in the sport.

The most practical way to get your dog to swim is simply to have it retrieve objects from a lake or other suitable body of water. Common sense dictates that you should avoid water that is polluted, dangerously cold, excessively turbulent, or which does not provide easy access to shore.

Dogs generally like to jump hurdles (reasonable ones, at any rate), so it shouldn't be too difficult to engage your pet in this activity. Begin by fashioning some kind of barricade (don't overdo it), and, with your pet attached to its leash, running up to the obstacle so the animal has no choice but to leap over it. Give the jump command just before it takes to the air. Repeat this exercise a few times, then remove the leash and have your Doberman sit in front of the barricade. Now move around to the opposite side, and see if you can urge the animal to perform on voice command alone. Should it walk around the obstacle instead of jumping over it, calmly return it to the starting line and try again. Eventually it will succumb to your wishes, at which time you will have the option of combining hurdle jumping with retrieving exercises for more demanding workout sessions (see page 49).

If you'd like to try jogging with your pet—which basically amounts to forced running on a leash, unless you're in a fairly secluded area—a few precautions are in order. In the first place, puppies and older dogs are not suited to this activity, and even healthy dogs in their prime should not be run for more than a couple of miles. Human runners who experience occasional pain or discomfort on an "off" day know enough to stop and rest or quit the day's outing altogether; a dog running with its master, however, can't or possibly won't communicate physical difficulties it may be experiencing, perhaps resulting in more serious problems later on.

Exercise and Aging

Puppies get all the exercise they need just being puppies; older dogs, however, have special needs. For one thing, they are less resistant to wet and cold weather. For some dogs, that means providing a coat or sweater—something that protects the chest, back and stomach or at least a thorough drying if you've been caught in a downpour.

It goes without saying that an older Doberman prefers a slower pace in life. With that thought in mind, do not be surprised if it shuns the advances of puppies and children. Rescue your aging pet if you see that it is getting annoyed with them.

Do not, however, let yourself confuse old age with lethargy. Some dogs, like some people, are just plain lazy when it comes to exercise. Don't neglect your health responsibilities to your pet just because you have its silent approval to do so. You should still exercise the rascal by taking it out for regular walks.

Training

Training your Doberman—at least to the point that it will respond to basic commands and understand the limits of acceptable behavior—is crucial to the quality of the relationship the animal will develop with you and your family. In a broader sense, it can also affect the animal's very survival among human society.

Obviously, a pet that constantly misbehaves—destroying furniture, for example, intimidating friends, or continuously disobeying commands—is liable to become a source of escalating frustration and unhappiness, inevitably compromising its status as a valued member of the household.

Unruly and vicious dogs that go so far as to attack innocent people and/or other animals can likewise cause a lot of grief—for all concerned. Besides the needless pain and suffering they may cause others, they also expose themselves to all kinds of injuries (accidental or otherwise) and, in extreme cases, to the long arm of the law. As a practical matter, owners of such dogs may be subject to costly lawsuits if their pets hurt someone. That's understandable, because more often than not, the root of the problem turns out to be improper handling and careless or insufficient training. The simple truth is, dogs are not born "mean" or "bad"; neglect and mistreatment make them so.

Certainly in the case of large and powerful breeds like the Doberman, which are physically capable of inflicting serious—under extreme circumstances, even life threatening—injuries, the parameters of acceptable behavior must be well defined, and they must be maintained with absolute consistency.

Training is more than a preventive measure, however. The very process, if conducted properly, stimulates the animal's intelligence. It also builds and strengthens the personal bond between dog and owner. These are welcome benefits to be sure, but they require judiciously executed input on the part of the trainer. There's a right way—and many wrong ways—to go about it.

Repetition Is the Key

Essentially, training consists of establishing a series of conditioned reflexes in your pet. The way to do this is through repetition, as much as it takes to form the right habits. The degree to which you are successful depends as much on the animal's attention and concentration as it does on your own enthusiasm. That's why it's best to keep training sessions brief—no more than 10 or 15 minutes at a time, at least at the outset.

The potential for success is also greatly influenced by the animal's age. Contrary to the popular adage, you *can* teach an old dog new tricks; it's the young ones you'll most likely have problems with. A puppy isn't ready for any meaningful training until it reaches at least ten weeks of age, and even then its learning ability is still limited.

One has to start somewhere, of course. A logical first step is to teach the animal its name. Continuous use of it when you address your pet will get the concept across in due time. Although a dog will naturally tend to approach you when you call its name, you will still want to teach it to come to you on command.

As with all other training, this requires a calculated degree of persistence on your part. Begin by coaxing the animal with your voice. It may help to squat down to the animal's eye level and reach out your hand to communicate the message. In most cases, the dog will respond to such devices, even if it's purely out of instinct. Eventually—that is, with practice—the animal will understand what "come" means when you say it, reacting accordingly.

My tip: At some point, your pet may test your will by not responding to—that is, intentionally ignoring—your command to present itself, perhaps because something of interest is distracting it at the time. Do not let such a challenge to your authority, however insignificant it may seem at the time, go unnoticed. This only serves to reinforce in the animal's mind that it can disregard you and have its way when it wants to—an undesirable precedent, to be sure, especially when you stop to consider that the command may in some situations be necessary to keep it out of danger.

Dealing with Disobedience

If your pet chooses to disobey you, use your tone of voice to communicate your displeasure. Do so immediately, as dogs have a rather short attention span and will not understand what they are being scolded for if you wait too long.

Never use violence—or even the threat of it—to mold a dog's behavior. Animals so conditioned can develop vicious tendencies, or else they may become timid, cowering at their owner's every move. Neither behavior is

desirable, and both can be difficult to correct. So put away those rolled-up newspapers and those menacing straps! The idea of wielding such props to intimidate your pet—even if you have no intention of actually using them—is without merit. Aside from an occasional slap on the butt to get its attention, the only time you should even *consider* hitting your dog is if it is threatening to bite you.

It also does no good to punish your dog by withholding food, water, shelter, or other basic necessities. Aside from being cruel and reprehensible, it serves no useful purpose in the training process.

Praise Gets Results

You're likely to get infinitely better results training your Doberman with lots of praise given lovingly and generously whenever it does something right. It will then be more inclined to respond favorably to future training efforts.

You can help maintain this productive arrangement by avoiding calling your pet when you want to reprimand it for some improper behavior. Under such circumstances, it's better that *you* approach your dog to voice your complaint, the logic being that the animal should always associate coming to you as a positive, rewarding experience, never as a potential source of displeasure.

In spite of your best efforts, there are bound to be failures and setbacks, especially in the beginning. Be patient with your Doberman, and above all, be consistent in your leadership. For example, it you do not want your dog to climb on furniture or stand around the dinner table begging for handouts, don't make an exception just because you have guests in the house. Allowing "special" circumstances to negate whatever rules of conduct you are trying to establish is, to say the least, counterproductive.

Sooner or later, you will probably discover that your Doberman responds to commands with more vigor and enthusiasm when you are dangling a piece of food or a dog treat before its eyes. Don't overdo it. There's nothing wrong with giving your pet a snack every now and then, but it should never come to rely on such inducements. Your dog must learn to respond to *you*, not to its own weaknesses.

Saying "No"

Another basic command you will probably introduce early and use often—is "no!" With a puppy in the house, you'll have plenty of opportunities to practice the word as the animal explores both its new home and the limits of your own tolerance. Always say the command with authority, and say it loudly and sharply enough to communicate the urgency of your message, but omit anger and other emotions from your voice; they will only distract the animal.

It's also recommended that you follow up the verbal reprimand with some kind of corrective action that will help your Doberman understand what it did to initiate this response from you. For example, if the animal is chewing on a shoe, snatch it away; if it's menacing your cat, take it into the next room.

Housebreaking

No doubt your most urgent initial training goal will be to housebreak your new pet. There are two basic methods of accomplishing this objective, depending to some degree on personal preference, but more so on your living situation.

If you own a home, you can either paper-train your puppy indoors first, waiting until it has grown a bit before introducing it to the practice of doing its business outdoors; or you can skip paper-training, concentrating on the

Five-week-old Doberman pinscher puppies exploring their litter box.

outdoors approach from the outset. Although the latter method is generally preferred because it is less involved, neither is completely foolproof or accident free.

If you're an apartment-dweller, you may not have such easy access to the outside, in which case you probably have no choice but to paper-train your pet, waiting until the animal develops better control of its bowel and bladder before making the transition to the outdoors. Typically, that won't happen until your Doberman is around four months old.

Whichever method you choose, it's best to restrict the puppy to a single room during the house-breaking phase. The kitchen seems ideal, if only because there's no carpeting to worry about when the inevitable "accident" occurs, making clean up easier, and also because, in most living quarters, that's where the back door is.

You may at first feel a little uneasy about bearing the brunt of housebreaking in your food preparation area, but there's no need to fear contamination of food as long as normal cleaning schedules and hygienic common sense prevail. As far as the potential for the animal constantly begging for food is concerned, this is a situation you will have to deal with sooner or later anyway—never fear, it is a correctable behavior. And don't forget that, unless your kitchen is very small, you also have the option of cordoning off a section of it, restricting access to areas where you want greater freedom of movement without worrying about your Doberman getting underfoot. The animal will still enjoy the security of your presence, as well as the social benefits of frequent contact with members of the household.

Speaking of security, before you restrict your Doberman to its initial living space, inspect the area carefully, removing or neutralizing any items that may cause harm to the animal, or which may be in any way damaged by it. Puppies are inclined to chew, climb, or paw at almost anything that strikes their attention, so caution is very much in order. Watch for sharp edges, electrical cords that can be gnawed, poisonous materials that could be ingested, furniture or furnishings that can tip over or fall, and any other pitfalls you can imagine. As for items that your puppy might damage, the list includes shoes, clothing, rubber, leather, wood, paper, or plastic—actually, just about anything, if your pet can get the right grip on it. So play it safe!

Line the pup's entire living space with newspaper. That will make it easier to clean when it relieves itself. Even if you take the animal outside frequently, there are bound to be occasions when you've missed your cue (if indeed one was given). Replace paper as needed.

The Paper-Training Phase

As the animal emerges from infancy, it will probably begin to relieve itself in the same general location of its living space each time. Once you have determined the approximate spot your pet seems to favor, you can begin to paper-train it. The idea is to *gradually* remove small sections of the floor covering, beginning with those areas farthest away from the animal's "drop zone," exposing an ever-increasing amount of bare floor. As long as the animal continues to direct its efforts to the area of its living space that is covered with newspaper, keep reducing the size of that area over a period of several weeks until it measures no larger than about three square feet. Give the dog lots of praise whenever it performs to expectations and hits the target, and if you feel some additional prompting may be in order, leave a bit of previously soiled paper on top of each new arrangement of floor covering. It will not go unnoticed, serving as a subtle reminder of purpose and availability.

When a "mistake" occurs and you are there to witness it, chastise the animal, but only with your voice. Don't *ever* rub its face in the mess. Contrary to popular belief, such a reaction will do nothing to expedite training; in fact, it can only complicate the task. Backtrack a little, widening the spread of newspaper somewhat if you think you may have proceeded with training too quickly, but continue towards your ultimate goal.

Should the misdeed occur while you are away, it won't do much good to scold the dog on your return. By that time, the animal will have difficulty associating your displeasure with the action that prompted it, so it's unlikely there is a lesson to be learned.

If the animal makes a mess when it is outside of the temporary living space you have provided—while you are playing with it, for example, or when it is being let outside (or on its way back in)—you will want to clean the spot thoroughly, of course, but don't stop there. If any trace of waste remains, even so little as to escape detection by a *human* nose, it's not improbable that your pet will return to the site, given the chance. Use a disinfectant or one of the special odor eliminators sold in pet stores to make sure no scent remains. If you're in a pinch, even a small dose of ground pepper may deter a return engagement.

As your Doberman grows and acquires better control of its bodily functions, it will need to relieve itself less frequently. The likeliest times will probably be after eating, sleeping, or playing. Now you can start taking the animal outside, praising it profusely when it does its business there. Returning to the same location at pretty much the same time every day will enhance the chances of continued success.

As the training progresses, you can begin to remove the last of the newspapers from the floor of your home. Soon the barrier that contains the animal can be removed as well, though you may still want to restrict your pet's access to certain areas of the home when you are asleep or away.

Even a fully grown dog may need to "go out" as many as four times a day; younger ones may need relief as often as every two or three hours. You'll have to accommodate these schedules as best you can. There's more to it than watching the clock, of course. That's why it's also important to learn to recognize the warning signals that mean the animal is ready to do its duty. It may start sniffing at corners and turning around in circles, barking at the back door, looking for newspaper on the floor, or staring at you intently with that unmistakable look on its face. Don't bother second-guessing—grab your coat and go.

During the transition stages of training—that is, when you remove the last

A puppy will regard a crate as its den—a safe and comforting place that is to be kept clean. For this reason it can be used as a training aid; but you must take your pet out regularly and watch carefully for signs of distress.

of the dog's floor covering and begin to channel its elimination needs to the great outdoors—many trainers recommend chaining or otherwise restricting the dog to its bed at night, since it will be reluctant to make a mess there. If you try this method, be sure to let the animal out just before bedtime and as soon as possible in the morning.

The Direct Approach

Direct housebreaking, in which you attempt to circumvent the paper-training phase, still requires restricting the animal for the first few weeks to an enclosed area covered with newspapers. The only difference is that you will try to anticipate your pet's need to relieve itself by taking it outside as often as possible during the course of each day, encouraging it from the start to do its duty there.

Note, however, that the direct approach requires a little more effort

When a dog "heels" it walks at the left side of its trainer. It should not lunge forward or lag behind.

The "stay" command orders your Doberman to remain still wherever it is.

The object of the command "come" is to have your dog come running whether it wants to or not.

on your part. To maximize the benefits of training, it's important that you—or someone—be available to let the dog outside with reasonable frequency (especially after playing, sleeping, or eating). Otherwise, the animal will have no choice but to relieve itself inside the home. And while it is inevitable that such incidents will occur now and then, they break the cycle of the habit you are trying to establish. The less that happens, the better.

As the weeks of training and positive reinforcement pass by, your dog's toilet habits will become fairly predictable. As in the paper-training method, that's when you can do away with the barricade that separates the animal from the rest of the family.

Basic Training

Preliminaries

At around six or seven months of age, your Doberman will be ready to proceed with more serious training. If you haven't already done so, now's the time to purchase a training collar and lead and get the animal accustomed to them.

Despite the unflattering name by which they are known, so-called "choke" collars, designed to constrict with increasing pressure, are generally acknowledged as best for training purposes, provided they are used properly—meaning tactfully and without malice.

The way to begin is to put the collar around the Doberman's neck so it has a chance to get used to its weight and feel. Because the animal will always walk on your left during training, make sure the loose ring of the collar is positioned on the right side of its neck, where the lead will attach to it.

After the dog has worn the collar for a day or two, you can introduce it to the leash. Take the animal into the backyard, affix the leash to the collar, and let it run around with it for a while. Next, take hold of the leash and try "walking" the animal, applying as little pressure as possible to the choking mechanism.

Don't be discouraged if things don't go too smoothly at first. With frequent practice and accompanying praise—the animal will learn to follow your movements at a pace and position that offer minimum resistance. At that point, whenever your Doberman begins to stray from your control, a quick, gentle tug on the leash will usually suffice to correct the behavior.

Occasionally, a stronger response may be called for, but be careful not to hurt the animal by misusing the device, applying the choke mechanism unrelentingly or with brutal force. In the wrong hands, a choke collar can indeed become an instrument of torture. Your pet shouldn't run away and hide every time the collar and leash come out of storage; on the contrary, the animal should react with enthusiasm, equating them with the welcome opportunity to go out for a walk and to enjoy the company and attention of its master.

When teaching your Doberman to heel, remember to give lots of praise when it performs well.

Heel!

The next logical step is to teach the Doberman to heel on command. There's no quick and easy way to do this; it's simply a matter of conditioning—repeating the motions until they become second nature and, as always, praising the animal generously whenever it performs to expectations.

With the dog positioned on your left side, start to walk forward, calling your Doberman's name, followed by the "heel" command, at the same time giving the leash a gentle tug to prompt the animal's movement. Continue moving forward, trying to keep the animal's neck and shoulder area at a fairly constant distance opposite your left leg. As the dog speeds up or falls behind, give the leash a light snap and repeat the "heel" command, praising the animal when it lines up with you again.

It will take time before the lesson is fully learned, so be patient, limiting practice sessions to no more than two a day. Eventually, you'll notice that your Doberman has begun to heel on command alone. Then you can start on more advanced maneuvering, such as 90- and 180-degree turns and other, more complicated drills. Having mastered these, your dog will be an infinitely more bearable walking companion. The ultimate test is to have your Doberman heel off its leash, but don't proceed to this level of training until the animal has fully mastered heeling while still attached to its reins.

Although you can safely begin increasing training periods to as much as half an hour as the animal gets older, be sure to allow time to play with your pet whenever you take it outdoors for training—preferably *after* "school" is out. It serves as a kind of reward for its learning efforts and ends the day's lessons on a pleasant, happy note.

Sit!

Teaching your pet to sit on command is the next step. In obedience training, dogs in the heel position are taught to sit automatically whenever their handlers stop walking. You can teach your dog to do this without monumental effort. As you walk the dog in the heel position, stop every so often, giving the "sit" command each time. Demonstrate the desired response by gently pushing your Doberman's rear down into a sitting posture, at the same time using your other hand to keep the animal's head up and facing forward in the appropriate heel position.

Repeat this procedure continuously, with the usual dose of praise, and before long your pet will begin responding to your voice command alone. By that stage, you can make the dog sit virtually anytime, simply by voicing the command. Any lapse in performance

To teach the "sit" command, gently push the dog's rear down while using the other hand to keep its head up and facing foward.

can be easily corrected by repeating the command as you physically place the animal into position. Eventually, you won't even have to tell your Doberman to sit when the two of you are out walking and you come to a halt. It will usually do so on cue.

Stay!

Next on the agenda of basic commands is "stay." Begin by having the dog assume the sit position. Holding the leash in one hand, raise the palm of the other in front of its face to hand signal the command as you say it. Having done so, step away from the animal as much as the leash allows, being careful not to exert any pressure on it that the dog may interpret as a signal to come forward. If your Doberman follows you anyway, give it a sharp "no" and start the exercise over again, using a free hand to hold it in place for a moment if necessary to help get the message across.

After your pet has learned to respond to the "stay" command on the leash, see if it will follow the same instructions without it. Gradually increase both the distance you move away from the animal and the length of time you maintain the command until you can safely keep the dog in position for two or three minutes, even at considerable distance.

Down!

Teaching your Doberman to lie down on command follows a similar pattern. Again, start with the dog in a sitting position. As you give the command "down," ease the animal into a prone position, either by pushing down on its shoulders, lifting its front legs down and forward, or some combination of the two.

Once it has assumed the correct position, hold the dog there for a moment, at the same time giving the "stay" command, which it has already

As you practice the "stay" command, gradually increase the distance you move away from the animal and the length of time you maintain the command.

learned. Repeat the exercise several times during consecutive training sessions until the animal obeys you on voice command alone.

When your pet has learned the basic commands—come, heel, sit, stay, down—and can be relied upon to respond to each of them without fail or hesitation, preliminary training is complete. Certainly there is much more your Doberman can be taught, but with these initial hurdles behind you, you can at least feel secure that the prescribed foundations have been established.

Additional Training

Dealing with Problems

Even after the essentials have been mastered, be prepared to deal with special problems that may manifest themselves from time to time. The list includes excessive barking, biting, jumping on people, climbing on furniture, begging, and food stealing.

Excessive barking: As dog owners, we can all appreciate a pet that promptly alerts us to the approach of strangers, but a dog that barks without end—even at the slightest provocation—can become a terrible nuisance, both to you and to your neighbors. Whenever your Doberman gets out of hand in this area, give it a firm "no" to quiet it down, demonstrating that there are definite limits to your tolerance of its vocal bravado.

If it persists in its noise making, confine it to a room, responding to any subsequent outbreaks by knocking loudly on the door and reprimanding it without actually entering the room—that is, unless its vocalizations seem especially urgent or frenzied. What you want to avoid is giving the animal the false notion that you will come to it immediately every time it starts to "sing."

Jumping on people: Should the animal get into the habit of jumping on you (and everyone else) to get attention, simply give the "down" command, which it is already familiar with. If the

If your pet picks up the bad habit of jumping up on people, use your knee to gently knock it off balance. After a few such episodes, the dog will probably discontinue the practice.

animal does not curtail the behavior, try raising your knee when it leaps up so that you gently knock it off balance. After several such episodes, it will decide that this is not a practical way to greet you when you come home.

Climbing on furniture: Repetitive reprimands will also teach your Doberman that it is not a welcome guest on beds and sofas. If you discover that the animal sneaks onto furniture when you are away, you can place sheets of crackly paper (or a suitable substitute) on it, hoping the sound will deter it from doing so. If that doesn't work, there is little alternative but to deny the animal access to those rooms.

Begging: To deal with begging at the dinner table, all you need do is say "no," ordering your Doberman to lie down if its bed is nearby. At the outset, you may have to repeat the exercise every time you sit down to eat, but the dog will get the message eventually, especially if you allow no lapse in this rule. If you want to give the animal some table scraps occasionally, take the treats to its food bowl.

Stealing food: Restricting the dog's intake of food in this manner will also help deter food stealing from tabletops and kitchen counters. The animal must learn that this is strictly forbidden, and a stern reprimand is in order if you catch it in the act. The concern here is not so much that your Doberman will devour your dinner—it shouldn't be accessible anyway—but that it may someday ingest contaminated or otherwise harmful foods, perhaps with tragic consequences.

Biting: If you don't want your Doberman to be a biter, don't ever encourage it to do so, even in play. If the dog does nip at you, voice your displeasure loudly, forcing its jaws shut for several seconds or lightly slapping it on the muzzle if sterner measures are called for. When the dog submits

48

to your correction, praise and pet it briefly to show that you harbor no bad feelings about the incident.

My tip: No dog should ever intentionally bite its master, but don't test this principle to excess by teasing the animal, especially when it is eating. Even your pet has its limits.

Retrieving

One of the nonessential but potentially useful and/or entertaining skills you may want to add to your pet's repertoire is retrieving. Most dogs take to this activity naturally, eagerly chasing down virtually anything you throw in their direction. Getting the object back, however, is not always so easy. Ideally, you want the animal to not only secure the item in question, but also to bring it back to you, dropping it directly into your hands.

Whether you prefer to use "fetch" or "get it" or some other choice of words, try to give the same command each time during retrieving exercises, at

To teach your pet to surrender an object, start with the familiar commands of "sit" and "stay," then take the item from its mouth as you voice instructions to "let go" or "drop it."

Only after your dog has mastered the basic commands—sit, stay, come, heel and lie down—should you proceed to more advanced levels of training.

least in the beginning. Mixing commands may confuse the animal.

Your Doberman will naturally tend to bring its prize back towards your general vicinity, if for no other reason than to have you continue the "game," but in its excitement and playfulness, it may hesitate in relinquishing it. If that's the case, give the by now familiar commands to "sit" and "stay," then approach the animal, taking the object from its mouth as you introduce a new command: "drop it" or "let go." If it still resists in some manner—growling or turning away from you—give it a stern "no" to communicate your dissatisfaction. As always, performance will improve with practice and praise.

"Shaking Hands"

Most dog owners inevitably get around to teaching their pets to "shake hands." An easy lesson to teach, it merely involves having the dog sit in front of you, stating the desired command, and taking the animal through the motions by picking up its paw and "pumping" it briefly. With frequent repetition, your pet will start to respond to your verbal command alone, but don't be surprised if it occasionally offers its paw even when you don't ask for it.

Staying Alone

A more practical lesson you can impart on your pet, preferably when it is still a puppy, is staying home alone. This is more a matter of conditioning than actual training, but it is a valuable lesson nonetheless. Some dogs left alone for the first time don't handle it very well; beset with anger or fear, they may bark and howl to the point of aggravating your neighbors, or they may take off on a rampage inside your home, destroying anything and everything they can get their teeth and paws on.

You can do something to stem such unpleasantness by occasionally isolating your Doberman for short but increasing periods of time in an area of your home where it cannot hear or see you (in a spare room if you have one), but where you can still monitor any major disturbances that may occur. This will help the dog become acclimated to periods of solitude; it will also give you an insight into how much difficulty—if any—your pet is likely to give you in this area of behavior. Be sure to fashion a bed for the animal, provide water and perhaps a toy or treat or two, and secure the premises as best you can. See how the Doberman takes to this confinement, and of course, praise it heartily on your "return."

Advanced Training

If, during the course of your training efforts, you've discovered that both you and your Doberman have developed a genuine zeal for such work, perhaps you will consider continuing your efforts on a higher plane of achievement.

For example, when the animal can heel (both on and off its leash), and will come, sit, lie down, and stay on command, in addition to being able to stand for inspection by a judge, it can earn its "Companion Dog" title (Novice Class) by simply demonstrating these skills at an officially sanctioned obedience trial. Your local breed club or the American Kennel Club can provide you with the details on these regularly scheduled events.

They can also help you with the special training your pet needs—including directed jumping, scent discrimination, and hand-signal work—for more advanced testing.

The ultimate in canine scholarship, though not required or even highly

The Doberman pinscher makes an excellent and incorruptible watchdog. However, very solid professional training is essential. Your local club can provide you with further details. Under no circumstances should you consider undertaking this kind of training by yourself.

recommended for family dogs, is guard dog training, culminating in official guard dog trials. Here you will undoubtedly need professional assistance, as the dog will have to learn to deal with simulated attacks, fleeing "criminals," and similar scenarios.

If, like most pet owners, your training needs are of a more basic variety, don't overlook the obedience classes sponsored by local dog clubs, animal organizations, and even private tutors in your community. The cost for such classes are often quite reasonable, and even though you may be sharing the forum with a few dozen other dog owners, you'll still have ready access to the knowledge and guidance of an expert. As an added benefit, such regular gatherings will also help your Doberman become accustomed to interacting with people—and other dogs.

While an experienced trainer can prove to be an invaluable ally in your teaching efforts, keep in mind that, when all is said and done, the brunt of the job rests squarely on you.

Travel by Car

There will likely be occasions when you'll want to take your pet with you when you are going away—be it on vacation, or even just across town. There are rules of conduct that apply here as well, but they are primarily meant for *you*, the owner.

As we all know, dogs (most of them, anyway) love to stick their heads out of car windows to take in the full excitement of passing images and to wallow in the sensation of movement. It's hard not to indulge them in this simple pleasure, but the fact of the matter is that such behavior can prove harmful to them. Even if you feel confident that your Doberman will not—or cannot, because of physical restraints—fall out or foolishly be tempted to jump out of the moving vehicle, as dogs have been known to do, there is still the very real and entirely unpredictable possibility that the animal can sustain an eye injury or ear problem from prolonged exposure to high-velocity wind.

When driving longer distances by car, it's best to keep the animal confined to a comfortable and properly sized cage or crate that your car can accommodate. If, heaven forbid, you are involved in an accident, such containers improve the odds that the dog will escape serious injury. Under normal driving conditions, they will also keep the animal from jumping around and distracting or disturbing you, if it is so inclined.

The same rules apply—only more stringently so—for people who transport their pets in the back of pickup trucks. Never do so unless the animal is in a cage or crate of some kind, or at least is attached to one of several specially designed harnesses (available in most pet stores) made specifically for such use. A standard leash is *not* sufficient to control the animal properly, and having no restraints at all is tantamount to criminal negligence. Many dogs have been killed as a result of such carelessness.

Finally, although you've probably heard it before, a few additional rules bear repeating. Try not to leave your Doberman in the car unattended, especially in warm weather when the rays of the sun can quickly turn it into a blazing oven. Even if you park in the shade and leave the windows partially open, the sun's movement can chase away protective shadows in a relatively short amount of time. Make your absences as brief as possible and, when delayed, check on the animal with regular frequency.

Ailments and Injuries

Dogs are subject to a vast array of illnesses and injuries during the course of their lives. How we respond to these health problems—and the measures we take to prevent them—can greatly influence both the animals' longevity and, equally important, the basic *quality* of their lives.

For the individual owner, the best advice one can give is know your Doberman—and your veterinarian. Health care starts with you. If you take an honest and genuine interest in your pet—not just feeding, grooming, and exercising it regularly, but also making the extra effort to observe its movements, mannerisms, and temperament, and give it a physical inspection now and then—you will be able to notice problems more quickly when they arise. Sometimes, that can mean the difference between life and death.

Many serious infectious diseases are preventable through routine vaccination.

Recognizing Symptoms

It's not as important that you are able to diagnose a particular disease or injury as it is that you recognize the symptoms. The rest, in most cases, you should leave to your veterinarian.

Of course, there may be problems whose symptoms are not so readily discernible. That's why you must keep your Doberman on a regular vaccination schedule, and bring it in for regular checkups at least once a year; more often when it reaches its senior years.

Most signs of trouble should be fairly obvious. The list includes fever, coughing, extreme loss or gain of appetite or weight, shivering, constipation, chronic diarrhea, abnormal stools, increased urination, labored breathing, lameness or paralysis, frequent vomiting, open wounds, hair loss, skin inflammations, unusual drooling or discharges, seizures, badly swollen joints or muscles, an awkward gait, bizzare behavior in general, loss of coordination, and obvious signs of pain. Any one of these symptoms should prompt, at the very least, a phone call to your veterinarian who will advise you of the best immediate course of action. This may or may not include bringing the animal in for immediate medical attention.

Serious Diseases

What infectious diseases like distemper, rabies, hepatitis, leptospirosis, parvovirus, and tracheobronchitis (kennel cough) all have in common—besides the fact that they are caused by tiny organisms that invade the animal's body—is that all are preventable through routine vaccination.

Distemper

While distemper was once considered one of the deadliest of canine diseases, today only nonimmunized dogs are likely to contract it. The virus enters the body via the mucous membranes. In most cases, it is passed directly through one dog to another, but it can also be transmitted through hair brushes, blankets, or even items of clothing that have been exposed to the virus.

Symptoms include fever, dry cough, diarrhea, vomiting, and a watery discharge from the eyes and nose. A puppy or young dog would appear exhausted; its appetite would become almost nonexistent. In advanced cases, muscle cramps and loss of equilibrium are likely to occur as well. In puppies, the disease is almost always fatal; in older dogs, permanent damage to the nervous system is likely.

Rabies

Dangerous both to nonimmunized dogs and humans alike, the rabies virus enters the body through bite wounds inflicted by an already infected animal. As the virus spreads, a series of changes begins to occur in the newly stricken victim. First, the animal displays otherwise unexplainable mood swings, vacillating from irritability to affection. It also appears especially sensitive to noise and light, and it's not uncommon for rabid dogs to attempt to eat undigestable things like wood or even pieces of stone, all the while refusing to partake of normal food. In advanced stages, symptoms include attacking and biting, frenzied running, difficulty in swallowing, and uncontrollable drooling. During the final stages, the animal's body becomes completely paralyzed; convulsions and death soon follow.

Any person bitten by a dog suspected to be rabid must report the incident to a physician as soon as possible. Previous treatments required a series of at least 21 shots over a 60-day period. Current treatment is far less severe, requiring only six or seven injections over a four-week period.

Hepatitis

An infectious disease of the liver, canine hepatitis is spread from dog to dog via saliva, urine, and contaminated objects. Symptoms include high fever, inflammation of nasal passages and pharynx, vomiting, diarrhea, and a painful inflammation of the liver that makes the area sensitive to the touch. This viral disease sometimes runs its

Taking your pet's temperature is not as difficult as it may seem. Have a helper restrain the animal while you slip the lubricated thermometer into its rectum, holding it in place for 2 or 3 minutes before removing it. The normal temperature range is between 99.5° and 101.5°(F), although puppies often surpass that mark, just as older dogs typically fall short of it.

course without perceptible symptoms, although in many such cases, the eventual result is clouding of the cornea or even total blindness.

Note: Infectious canine hepatitis is not the same as the hepatitis that afflicts humans. The canine variety is *not* contagious to people.

Leptospirosis

The bacteria that cause leptospirosis are passed in the urine of rats and mice. Dogs may be exposed to this disease by drinking contaminated water from ditches, puddles, or ponds. Symptoms typically include fever, loss of appetite, increased thirst, vomiting, stomach and intestinal disorders, and loss of consciousness. Eventually, jaundice sets in, and the animal begins losing weight. Infection of the kidneys, characterized by yellowish-

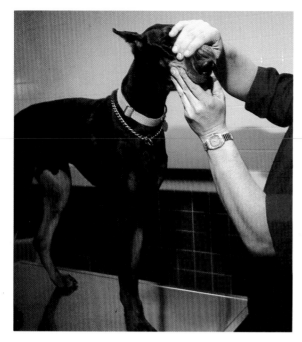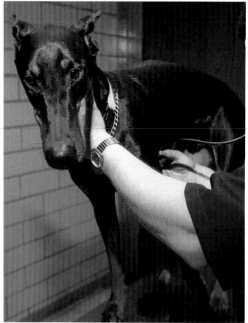

brown urine, typically follows. This condition, in turn, often leads to uremic poisoning. If the disease is diagnosed in the early stages, dogs that have not been immunized can be treated with antibiotics.

Parvovirus

Carried in the feces of infected dogs, parvovirus attacks not only the intestinal tract, but also the body's white blood cells and the heart. Conquering this disease can be difficult, for the virus is a hardy one, capable of surviving under a wide range of temperatures and conditions. Furthermore, direct contact with an infected animal is not the only way the virus is transmitted. It can also be carried on the hair and feet of stricken animals, and even on the shoes and clothes of people.

Symptoms appearing within a week of exposure include fever, vomiting, bloody urine, and severe diarrhea (gray or yellow-colored feces). Dehydration is swift, and death usually occurs within 72 hours. The virus is especially deadly to puppies, but whatever your Doberman's age, it's smart to keep it away from other dogs' wastes.

Tracheobronchitis

Dubbed "kennel cough" (much to the dismay of kennel operators, who understandably abhor the term), tracheobronchitis is a highly contagious airborne virus. Capable of spreading rapidly where large numbers of dogs are housed (hence the kennel connection, though in all fairness most kennels are extremely vigilant of this problem), the virus causes inflammation of the trachea and larynx, initiating the cough that is its namesake. A runny nose often accompanies these symptoms. While not normally a fatal disease, it can take a heavier toll on puppies and small dogs. Often, it leaves them

54

more susceptible to other infections. Inoculation is the only preventive measure, though it cannot be administered to pregnant females for fear of contaminating unborn pups.

Lyme Disease

This tick-borne disease named for the Connecticut town in which the ailment was first diagnosed in humans, has become increasingly prevalent as a threat to dogs and even more so to their human companions. Your pet should be examined for ticks regularly. If any are discovered, they should be removed promptly (see page 57). Should symptoms of Lyme disease occur (fever, painful swelling of the joints), prompt medical attention is required. A person who develops frequent headaches and the aforementioned symptoms should also seek medical attention. (Be sure to tell your physician that you have a dog and may have been exposed to ticks.)

Tetanus

Sometimes called lockjaw, tetanus is caused by poison-producing bacteria that thrive inside wounds where oxygen cannot penetrate. To safeguard against this disease, the animal should get an antitetanus shot from the veterinarian. Always clean and disinfect any wounds your Doberman may incur. Deep wounds should be treated by its veterinarian with a broad spectrum antibiotic.

Tonsillitis

This disease can be viral or bacterial. Not an especially serious problem, it can, however, be a symptom of a more serious affliction. Normally, the condition should run its course within a week. Symptoms include enlarged and reddened tonsils, poor appetite, a discharge from the eyes, and occasionally, vomiting. Consult your veterinarian if these symptoms appear.

Here a veterinarian performs a routine examination of a Doberman. From left to right: inspecting the mouth for tooth and gum disorders, checking the heart and respiratory system, examining the ears, checking the animal's weight.

Digestive Disorders

Vomiting is not unusual among puppies and young dogs, who often display poor eating habits (eating too much or too fast), but violent and frequent vomiting can indeed be a cause for alarm, as it can mean that the animal has ingested poison or some other foreign object, or that an infectious disease has attacked its body. Consult your veterinarian promptly.

Diarrhea, likewise, is a normal occurrence from time to time, but if it becomes a chronic condition, you should have your Doberman checked for worms.

Once again, the same logic applies to constipation problems. If the condition persists, re-evaluate your pet's diet, which may be too dry for its system. Under the worst possible scenario, continuous constipation can also be a signal that the animal has swallowed an indigestible foreign object, in which case surgery may be required.

Respiratory Infections

Infections of the larynx and trachea can be related to a variety of different

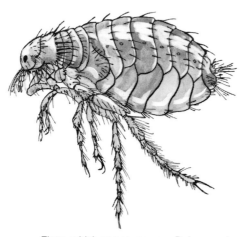

Fleas, which can cause your Doberman to scratch itself almost incessantly, also serve as intermediate hosts for tapeworms.

maladies—among them kennel cough and distemper, discussed earlier, and pneumonia. Symptoms of the latter include high fever, loss of appetite, lethargy, breathlessness and/or a rattling sound during breathing. Only a veterinarian can make an accurate diagnosis and prescribe the right treatment.

Although you should always turn to your veterinarian first there are at least two unrelated but major areas of health that will most certainly involve you and the rest of the members of your family. One is fleas and other external parasites; the other is the application of first aid during an emergency.

External Parasites

External parasites—particularly fleas, ticks, lice and mites—are more than a nuisance. In some cases, they can lead to health complications that can actually prove fatal to the animal. And even when they don't, they can make life miserable—both for the animal and its owners, who also fall prey to the ensuing plague.

While fleas, ticks, and lice in your Doberman's coat can be disposed of using one of the specially medicated shampoos, dips, and/or rinses available in pet stores, there remains the additional problem of dealing with the countless number of eggs the little monsters have likely left behind—in your pet's bedding and elsewhere. These can hatch days, even months later and start the problem all over again, just when you think your household has returned to normal. You should take precautions to prevent such an occurrence.

Reading directions carefully, treat your dog's bedding and all the carpets and public areas in your home with an appropriate insecticide, then vacuum thoroughly. Repeat this treatment in a week to ten days to finish off any survivors or new arrivals, at which time you should give your Doberman another treatment as well. In cases of extreme infestation, you may have to call in a professional exterminator to "de-bug" your home.

Fleas

Fleas, which can cause intense discomfort, also serve as carriers of tapeworm. Flea collars, sprays, and powders are a sensible way to prevent reinfestation of your pet, but such insecticide products should *not* be used on pregnant or nursing females or on puppies. They can harm them.

Ticks

Ticks are a major cause for concern since they can carry Lyme disease (see page 55), Rocky Mountain spotted fever, and encephalitis (inflammation of the brain)—among other diseases. They typically drop onto dogs from bushes and trees with which the animals come into contact. The pests feed on the dogs' blood—and sometimes on the blood of their owners! If you discover a tick attached to your pet, apply oil to it (or one of the specially formulated tick-removal products available at pet stores) so that it will suffocate and die. It can then be more easily removed with a pair of tweezers. Never pull on a tick, as its head may snap and remain imbedded in the skin, causing pain and inflammation. The correct method is to use a back-and-forth motion. Alternatively, you can dislodge ticks with a plastic credit card, using a sweeping action.

Mites

Producing a condition known collectively as mange, mites present a slightly different problem. There are so many different kinds—some of which are so small they can only be detected with a microscope—that it's best to let your veterinarian identify them and prescribe the proper treatment. Symptoms include shaking and

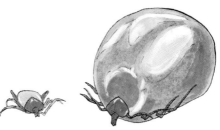

A tick before (left) and after (right) feeding.

scratching of the ears, as well as an accumulation of dark-colored ear wax (ear mites); intense itching and hair loss (white mites and red mites); and severe redness of the skin (chigger mites). Note that the white mite is also fond of human hosts. Left untreated, mange will spread.

Lice

You'll be able to spot these bloodsuckers on your Doberman's coat, but getting rid of them is not so easy. There are a variety of insecticides and specially formulated shampoos to kill lice, but treatment usually has to be

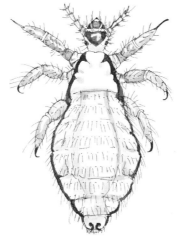

Careful examination of your Doberman's coat and skin is the best method to detect and identify external parasites such as the louse.

repeated several times in order to be fully effective.

Internal Parasites

Roundworms

The most common internal parasite, roundworms frequently invade the small intestine. White or yellow in color, they can grow to around four inches in length, causing a loss or marked increase of appetite, diarrhea, itching of the anal area, cramps, bloating of the stomach, a constant lack of energy, and paralysis. Especially dangerous to puppies, infestation occurs by way of worm eggs that already infected dogs pass in their stools—another good reason to keep your Doberman from investigating other dogs' droppings. Several different drugs are available to combat this problem. Most require denying food to the dog for 24 hours before administering the medication, repeating the treatment in another two weeks or so.

Tapeworms

This parasite also attacks the small intestine. Transmitted via such interme-

Tapeworms are never passed directly from one dog to another. The worms drop tail segments containing eggs and larvae that are subsequently consumed by fleas, lice, rabbits, pigs, or sheep. If a dog swallows one of these insect hosts, or if it eats meat contaminated with larvae, the parasites can pass into the small intestine where they develop into sexually mature tapeworms.

diary hosts as fleas, lice, rabbits, pigs, and sheep, the worms enter a dog's body in the form of larvae when the animal swallows one of the hosts or eats contaminated (improperly cooked) meat. Symptoms include weight loss, inflammation of the intestine, muscle cramps, itching of the anal area, and dullness of the coat. Worming medicines are readily available, but the best preventive measure is to avoid giving your pet uncooked meats and to keep its environment parasite-free at all times.

Heartworms

As the name suggests, this notorious parasite attacks the heart. As much as a foot in length (30.5 cm) when fully grown, it is chiefly transmitted by mosquitos that have themselves been infected after biting a dog carrying the worm. Symptoms are fatigue, nervousness, coughing, difficulty in breathing and, occasionally, swelling of the legs and feet. Treatment can only be trusted

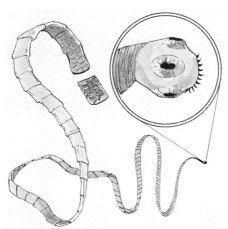

The long, segmented body of the tapeworm. The magnified head (insert) reveals the suckers with which the tapeworm attaches itself to the intestinal wall.

Although more than 11 years old when this picture was taken, this handsome former champion is living proof that the combination of regular exercise and a balanced diet—not to mention the attention of a loving family—contribute greatly to a dog's overall health and vitality.

To administer a pill or capsule, grasp the cheeks just behind the lip edges where the teeth come together on the inside of the mouth, and press inward as though squeezing. As the lips are pushed against the teeth, the pressure of your fingers forces the mouth open. Insert the medicine as far back on the base of the tongue as you can, pushing it back with your finger.

To encourage swallowing, raise your pet's head and massage its throat. When the tip of the animal's tongue shows between its front teeth, this usually suggests that medicine has been swallowed.

to an expert—in other words, a veterinarian—since it can have dangerous side effects, including suffocation (worms may retreat to the lungs, cutting off air) and blockage of blood vessels in the heart (after worms die).

Hookworms and Whipworms

Both of these parasites attack the intestines. They manifest many of the same symptoms as roundworms do, and in fact are eradicated using the same drugs. The former, especially, responds best with a diet heavy in liver and other meats, which an infected dog needs to build up strength. Both parasites serve to weaken the dog's body defenses, making it more susceptible to other physical problems.

First Aid

If your Doberman gets hurt while you are in a place where no help is readily available, its survival may depend on your knowledge of first aid.

Shock

A dog that has suffered severe trauma, for example, will frequently be unconscious. If that's the case, make sure that air passages are clear, and extend the animal's neck to facilitate breathing.

A state of shock often follows injury or severe fright. Symptoms include shallow breathing, a weak pulse, pale gums and dilation of the pupils. In extreme cases, failure of the circulatory system may follow. Immediate action dictates keeping your pet as quiet and still as possible—and covered, in cold weather—although your ultimate goal must be to get the animal to a hospital.

External Bleeding

If the dog is bleeding from a skin injury, wash the area with soap and water, then apply an antiseptic medication to the wound. If the injury is a large one and looks as though it will need stitches, apply a temporary gauze bandage, and immediately seek professional help.

To apply a bandage properly, place a thick layer of sterile gauze over the injured area, winding the bandage tightly enough to stop or at least slow down the bleeding. Remove the bandage periodically—every 15 or 20 minutes or so—to prevent excess swelling, and replace it with a new one if bleeding continues. Never apply cotton to a wound, as it may stick to it.

If a cut is deep and an artery has been severed, blood will appear bright in color, flowing in time with the heartbeat. Blood from a vein, on the other hand, will be a darker red. Its flow will be steady by comparison. To slow bleeding from an artery, apply pressure between the heart and the wound; where a vein is involved, pressure must be applied *below* the wound.

Internal Bleeding

Even if a dog appears to have survived an injury intact, it's still possible that the animal may have sustained internal damage. Signs of internal hemorrhaging include a loss of physical stability, the inability to move or stand up, and a pale gray discoloration of the gums. Bleeding from the nose may signify a head injury. If there is bleeding from the mouth, check both tongue and mouth for cuts. Whenever internal bleeding is suspected, quick veterinary assistance may prove critical to your pet's survival.

Broken Bones

Broken bones are fairly easy to diagnose, even for an amateur. Intense pain and loss of mobility are the prime indications. In the case of a compound fracture, you will be able to see the bone protruding through the skin. Keep the animal as still as possible, and fashion some kind of stretcher so you can transport it to the veterinarian with minimal discomfort.

A flat, hard surface makes the best improvised stretcher, but it's unlikely you'll find such an item when you need it most. You may have to make do with a blanket, tent, or other cloth-like material. Try to keep the surface taut. The animal should be subjected to as little movement as possible.

Sprains

Sprains and other serious injuries to muscles and ligaments may be mistaken for broken bones, the affected area becoming tender and swollen in much the same way. Emergency treatment is the same as for broken bones.

Dislocations

Dislocations—of the hip, knee, foot, or jaw—are likewise accompanied by swelling and loss of movement, and you may be able to detect the displaced bone with little effort. Do not, however, attempt to realign the bone yourself. Apply cold compresses to relieve pain, and seek medical assistance promptly.

Burns

Treatment of burns depends on the cause. Assuming the damage is confined to a small area (otherwise you'll definitely need professional help), burns caused by heat or fire can be treated by applying ice or cold water compresses, followed by a topical antibiotic. Do not use oily preparations. Burns caused by an acid or chemicals should be flushed with warm water, after which a solution of baking soda may be applied. Call your veterinarian for specific instructions; it will help greatly if you are able to identify the burn-causing agent.

Heatstroke

Heatstroke occurs when a dog is overexposed to the sun, overworked in hot weather, or, all too commonly, when it has been left too long in a car or other confined place that is hot and has insufficient air circulation. The animal will seem faint, and it may have difficulty breathing. Emergency treatment demands that you reduce its body temperature as quickly as possible. Place the animal in a tub or pool

Healthy Dobermans look elegant, strong and muscular, and keep a poker face that makes it difficult to read their moods!

filled with cold water, or soak it down with a garden hose, if one is handy. Your veterinarian will prescribe additional treatment.

Poisons

Poisons are another serious threat, for they exist in many places and in many forms. Symptom include shivering, panting, retching, vomiting, and, occasionally, convulsions. In extreme cases, coma and death may occur.

Unless you know what kind of poison the animal has ingested, you are at a disadvantage because emergency treatment varies. With most poisons, it's best that you induce vomiting, if it not already occurring. Mix equal parts of hydrogen peroxide and water (or two to three tablespoons of salt in a glass of water) and force the animal to drink it. This you can do by raising its head, pulling out the animal's lower lip to form a "gutter" of sorts, then pouring the mixture into it. Unfortunately, some poisons—such as gasoline, kerosene, and acids—can do as much damage coming out as they did going in, so forcing your Doberman to vomit is *not* recommended.

If you can identify the poison and its original container is within reach, it will likely have antidote instructions on the label. Consider yourself fortunate, but call the veterinarian as soon as possible anyway. If you suspect your Doberman has been poisoned but have no idea what specifically may have caused it, it may be wise to force vomiting anyway. The odds would seem in favor of such action, and failure to act could cost the animal its life.

Note that garden-variety pesticides can be poisonous to dogs. If you must use them around the home, do not let your dog come into contact with them for at least two weeks after application. And make sure that all chemicals, such as antifreeze, are stored where the animal cannot get at them.

Finally, while perhaps not a common occurrence, you should be aware that bee and wasp stings can cause adverse reactions in some dogs. Swelling, trembling, and, in extreme cases, circulatory failure, can result.

Seizures

There is little you can do if your Doberman suffers a seizure, except to restrain it gently and wait for it to pass. When the animal has recovered sufficiently, seek immediate medical attention.

Should your pet suddenly start choking and coughing, perhaps pawing at its mouth and shaking its head, it may very well have swallowed something that has become lodged in its throat. Open the dog's mouth, pull its tongue out a bit if you can grab hold of it, and see if you can spot the cause of the problem. If you see a foreign object in its throat, you can try to remove it if your fingers reach that far. If you can't get at it, rush the dog to the veterinarian—immediately!

Eye Injuries

For eye injuries—inflammations, cuts, scratches—wash the area with an eye lotion or boric acid solution (warm water is okay if neither are available), then dry carefully with gauze or a soft cloth. Apply eye ointment if you have it, and seek additional treatment.

Drowning

Contrary to what some people believe, not all dogs are great swimmers, and *any* dog can drown if it is forced to tread water past the point of exhaustion. To revive a dog so stricken, start by holding the animal up by its hind legs to remove some of the water in the lungs, then lay the animal on its side with its head and neck extended and its tongue pulled forward. Press down on its rib cage, releasing pressure every four or five seconds. If the dog doesn't recover quickly, try "mouth to nose" resuscitation. After making sure its throat is clear, close its mouth, take a deep breath and, covering the animal's nose with your lips, *gently* exhale, filling the dog's lungs with air—you'll know you're doing it right when you see its chest expand with your efforts. Repeat every five to six seconds. As soon as the dog recovers (one must always hope for the best), seek additional treatment.

Fish Hooks and Quills

Dogs that travel the backcountry sometimes bring home fishhooks and porcupine quills as souvenirs. A fishhook is rather easily removed. Use pliers or whatever facsimile you can devise to snip the barbed end (or the eye-end, if that will be easier) so you can pull the hook through the puncture without causing more damage—or pain! Apply an antiseptic and cover the wound with gauze, if that's practical. Porcupine quills are not so easy to extract, and it's likely you'll have more than one to contend with. What's more, quills tend to work their way deeper into the skin as time elapses, so prompt attention is required, especially if the chest area, where vital

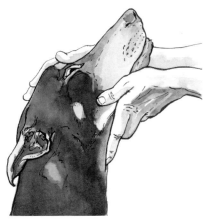

Inspect eyes frequently. If the dog seems to be blinking more than usual, or if the eyes are red or tear constantly, consult a veterinarian.

organs are located, has been affected. Your best course of action is to rush to a veterinarian, who can anesthetize your Doberman if there are many quills to remove.

If the accident occurs while you are far from "civilization," you may have to play doctor yourself—at least to clear the chest area. Start by cutting off the end of each quill. Because they are hollow, this will remove some of the pressure, making them easier to dislodge. Slowly twist out the quills (don't yank!), then apply antiseptic to the wounds. If medical assistance is anywhere within reasonable distance, have a professional finish the job. It's a painful process for your pet, and a little anesthesia may be, as the saying goes, just what the doctor ordered.

My tip: Your Doberman may be the love of your life, but if it becomes delirious or is suffering great pain, it may instinctively lash out at you while you are attempting to treat it. If someone else is with you, it will be easier to keep the animal under control; otherwise, you may have to muzzle the dog temporarily by tying a shirt-sleeve or whatever's handy around its snout.

Breeding

Unless you aspire to become a professional breeder, which most dog owners do not, the only good reason to breed a female Doberman is because you want an additional pet, and you prefer an offspring from the dog you already own and love.

Surely you wouldn't be doing it for financial gain. Considering the investment in both time and money to see such an undertaking through, you'd be lucky to break even.

The Perfect Mate

If you own a male Doberman, the incentive of offering it for stud service could very well be monetary, but unless your pet is a pedigreed show champion and/or a proven producer of championship-quality stock, don't expect the world to beat a path to your door. You've got *lots* of competition.

Nevertheless, whether your pet is male or female, if it is truly a fine and healthy specimen, it's just possible that you may some day seek or be offered the opportunity to mate it with a suitable partner. Before you jump at the chance, do some research. Find out exactly what's expected of you in such a venture, and satisfy yourself that you will be able to fulfill your part of the bargain thoroughly and honorably.

Don't even consider breeding your Doberman if it isn't of sufficient age. A male shouldn't be used for stud service until he is at least one year old. Females should not be mated until at least their second estrus (the peak of their sexual cycle), which typically translates to between fifteen and eighteen months of age. Occurring every

seven months or so, the estrus period lasts approximately nine days. It is the only time a female will accept the advances of a male.

Obviously, female dogs—and hence their owners—bear the brunt of breeding activity as it is they who must eventually contend with the pack of new arrivals and all the trials and tribulations that come with them.

The work will have started long before then, of course. Actually, one could argue that the most difficult, most crucial step of all in the entire breeding process is the very first one of all—that of finding that "perfect" mate. Professional breeders will go to great lengths—literally—to match their best dogs, often shipping them by air hundreds of miles (and farther) to produce what they hope will be improved stock.

As a novice breeder, you needn't go to such extremes, although you certainly have the option of doing so if you really do want to improve the bloodline and are willing to pay as much as several hundred dollars (or more) for professional stud service—not to mention the additional shipping charges involved (whatever the distance, it is customary to bring the female to the stud, as females tend to be less inhibited about being placed in a new environment).

No matter where you live, you can probably find suitable stud service within driving distance of your home, but considering that air transportation is both reasonably safe and inexpensive these days, you shouldn't have qualms about looking elsewhere if you're not satisfied with the selection of potential sires available to you.

If your ambitions are not quite so grand, you still have the alternative of seeking a pairing with a privately owned pet male of top quality and condition. Done properly, you should have every reason to expect handsome and healthy offspring of high if not exceptional quality.

So where do you begin your search? The avenues are many. For professional stud service, you might want to start with the breeder you bought your Doberman from—who no doubt will have suggestions. You can also consult your local or national breed club for prospects, or any of several dog magazines that carry such listings. For private-party arrangements, consult newspapers (you can even place an ad yourself), any other Doberman owners you may chance to meet, friends and acquaintances, and anyone else you can think of. You never know where such inquiries will lead you—perhaps to the sire of your dreams.

If you are indeed a novice, you would be wise to seek expert advice on analyzing pedigrees and tracing bloodlines of the studs you are considering. The idea is to compare puppies from backgrounds similar to your own's. If these have been of acceptable quality, there is at least a reasonable probability that your own efforts will be equally successful.

Breeding Strategy

Technically speaking, breeding strategy can take several different forms. Line-breeding, the recommended choice for the novice, is the pairing of two dogs of common but only distantly related ancestry (cousin to cousin, half-brother to half-sister, and so forth). A type of inbreeding, it is nevertheless considered the surest way to get offspring of predictable (as much as that is possible) quality.

Direct inbreeding (pairing father to daughter, brother to sister, and so forth) is unethical at best where it involves the

Young, healthy Doberman pinschers still have an air of innocence, but are far from timid!

mass production of animals purely for profit, but, under the right circumstances, it really can be used to enhance the physical attributes of a particular strain. Always a risky undertaking, this method should be left to experienced, professional breeders only.

Another form of breeding is known as outcrossing. The opposite of inbreeding, it attempts to enhance or correct physical features by pairing dogs of the same breed but of totally unrelated ancestry. While not as predictable as line-breeding, outcrossing can likewise produce the desired results.

Once you have a specific stud in mind, you would also be well-advised to solicit the help of someone who can properly evaluate the dog's physical appearance in relation to conformation standards of the breed. If you have elected to contact breeders in different parts of the country, you will have to rely on photographs to make a visual assessment of the animal, but you'll also get copies of the dog's pedigree to help you make your appraisal.

The owner of the stud will probably want to know about your own Doberman's health and temperament, and whether it, too, is free of serious faults. He or she may also ask you to submit *your* dog's pedigree, and, if this is a long-distance transaction, may likewise request that you send a photograph of the animal.

Arranging Transportation

If and when the deal is struck, contact the airlines that are most convenient for your pet's destination to find out about their procedures (and requirements) for handling dogs. Use direct flights whenever possible, and plan on shipping the animal one or two days prior to the onset of estrus. This is known as proestrus, typically lasting, like estrus itself, a period of nine days. If you are observant, you will recognize the start of the proestrus because the

dog's vulva will become swollen and the vagina will emit a bloody discharge. The female will not accept a mate during this initial phase.

If the stud you have selected is near enough for you to drive your pet to the location, you'll save a few bucks and spare the animal the inevitable if relatively minor discomfort of air travel. Here again, you'll want to coincide arrival between the tenth and fourteenth day after proestrus has begun.

Visiting the Veterinarian

Approximately one month before breeding, have your bitch examined by a veterinarian who will check for worms and other parasites, assess the animal's general health, and provide whatever vaccinations are called for (distemper, parvovirus and so forth), after which he or she will sign the health certificate you will need to present if the animal is traveling by air. This is also a good time to have the dog tested for brucellosis, a bacterial disease that can cause sterility and/or spontaneous abortion. Stud owners may require proof that the test was performed, but it's something you should have done anyway.

The Mating Ritual

Few people have never seen dogs in the act of mating. Essentially, the male mounts the female from behind, clasping her midsection with his front paws, then rapidly thrusts his pelvis back and forth until his seminal fluid has been discharged. Even after the act is completed, the animals will remain locked together physically—often rear to rear—in what is referred to as a "tie." Under no circumstances should you attempt to separate the animals; they will do so naturally in a short while.

Pregnancy

Pregnancy lasts about nine weeks, during which time you'll notice that the animal's weight and breast size gradually begin to increase, as will its appetite. Stick to your normal feeding regimen initially, but some time around the midway point you can start adding calcium and any other supplements your veterinarian may recommend to your pet's diet. At around seven weeks, you can start providing larger portions of food if the animal seems hungrier than usual, and a small daily serving of buttermilk should now be included as well. Noncultured milk may cause diarrhea.

Introduce your Doberman to its whelping box, which should be placed in a comfortably warm, somewhat secluded and draft-free area of the home, at least a week before the puppies are due. If you don't provide such a haven (it needn't be fancier than a box lined with newspapers, as long as it's big enough to accommodate mother and pups), your pet may choose to deliver its babies in your clothes closet or some equally inappropriate place.

Whelping

When the animal begins to refuse food and starts to pace around restlessly, that is a sign that the birthing period is approaching. Soon the dog's body temperature will begin to drop, and you may notice her shivering occasionally. Within 24 hours, labor can be expected to begin, at which time the animal will settle into its whelping box, panting heavily as the cervix expands and opens the birth canal. It's then that the puppies will start to arrive.

Each newborn is contained in a placenta membrane, which the mother must remove so the puppy can breathe. She will also sever the accompanying umbilical cord with her teeth. Most of the time, the mother will eat the placenta as she routinely cleans each arriving pup. Almost magically, the licking action stimulates the breathing process of the pups and brings the youngsters to life. (Defecation and urination must also be stimulated this way during the first few days of life.)

Once free of their mother's attention, the pups will instinctively seek a nipple to nurse on. If you can expedite the search, do so. Its important that every pup have some of its mother's milk during its first day of life, when its body is still able to absorb immunoglobulins—proteins in the milk that "immunize" the animal against various potential diseases (those that the mother is protected from).

Potential Complications

Most births occur without a hitch, but complications do arise from time to time. For example, a mother will sometimes neglect to remove a pup from its placenta, in which case your assistance will be required. You'll have no more than seven or eight minutes before the little one will suffocate.

Tear the sac open yourself, starting near the head, then wipe away the fluid from the animal's body, paying particular attention to clearing the nose and mouth. Placing the pup on a towel, massage its body lightly, but briskly, to duplicate the stimulus of the mother's licking action. If all goes well, it should soon begin breathing normally. Your job is finished after you cut the umbilical cord about two inches from the abdomen and tie it closed with a piece of string or strong thread. Dab some iodine on the end to protect against infection.

The same response may be necessary if a puppy is born feet first. Here, too, there is a risk that the animal may drown, so you'll have to act quickly. If it doesn't respond to body massage, your only other recourse is mouth-to-mouth resuscitation (cover its nose as you blow air down the throat). Alternate the two treatments for at least 15 minutes before giving up. Beyond that, there is virtually no hope of bringing it back to life.

If your pet seems to be having a little difficulty in delivering her offspring, you can sometimes help her by removing the pup yourself, if you know what you're doing. Using a clean towel, gently grab the pup as its mother is in the process of contracting. Be prepared to revive the newborn if its mother is slow to respond.

When To Consult Your Veterinarian

If you aren't able to assist and the mother continues to have labor difficulty, straining for several hours without delivering a pup, call your veterinarian for assistance. If the birth canal is blocked, the veterinarian may have to perform a cesarean section, removing the pups via the abdomen. Other danger signals to watch for include indications of extreme pain, continuous and uncontrollable trembling, or the passing of bloody or dark green fluid *before* any births occur.

Even if all has gone smoothly, you should still have a veterinarian inspect both mother and offspring within a day of the delivery. After that, there is not much more you can do until the puppies are three or four weeks old, other than keeping the whelping box clean and making sure that mother is being fed properly (two meals a day, plus frequent servings of buttermilk).

Sometimes the mother is unable to produce milk of her own initially. In that case, you will have to feed the animals by hand until she is able to take over naturally. You should also consult your veterinarian about this condition.

Females are naturally protective of their offspring, and it is rare for a mother to abandon her young.

Weaning

By the fourth week, it will be time to start weaning the puppies, that is, removing them from their mother's milk and on to solid food. Offer the youngsters small pieces of fresh (cooked) meat several times a day for the first few days, then switch to an appropriate puppy food, which you will have to serve four times daily until the animals are twelve weeks old, if you keep them that long.

As the weaning process is getting under way, keep the mother away from the puppies several hours each day, so they will gradually get used to her absence. By the fifth week, allow the mother to stay with her pups overnight, but only then. At six weeks, the youngsters should be completely weaned.

After weaning is completed, consult your veterinarian about testing for worms and scheduling the vaccinations that will be required.

By the eighth week, you can start placing the Doberman pups into what you can only hope will be loving homes. One way to help ensure that end is to begin making initial adoption inquiries as early as possible—even well before the pups are born.

These five-week-old puppies are enjoying their first solid food.

Understanding Dobermans

The Role of Instinct

Exactly how much of a dog's behavior is inherited and how much is learned is a debate that remains unsettled, except to say that both avenues of exchange seem very much involved. One expects a Doberman pinscher to be fearless and loyal, a "natural" watchdog, the same way one would expect a bird dog to take to water or a greyhound to running—in each case, such is the animal's "essence" as reinforced by generation after generation of natural and selective breeding.

Of course, not all dogs turn out the way we expect. Certainly those that have been mentally or physically abused or improperly trained or handled, can exhibit behavior extremes that exceed the bounds of normalcy. Our personal input as dog owners, therefore, is crucial—*especially* with an aggressive and powerful breed like the Doberman.

Taking an interest in your Doberman's behavior will go a long way in helping you establish and maintain a sound and happy relationship with the animal. Not only will it enhance your appreciation and enjoyment of your pet, it will also facilitate training and contribute to its long-term health—all very good reasons to make the effort.

Like virtually all other animals, dogs are motivated by instinct when it comes to basic matters of survival. Your family pet won't have to hunt for food like its counterparts in the wild, but it will reveal its ingrained sense of self-preservation in other ways—through sexual activity, expressions of territoriality, fighting, and other behaviors.

Many dogs, harking back to the pack-oriented social structure of their ancestry, have a tendency to dominate other animals (and people sometimes), instinctively competing for status and position. To be sure, certain breeds (the Doberman among them) exhibit this tendency more than others, and while some breeds seem not to show even a hint of such behavior, all engage in some form of ranking and/or assessment of their "peers."

The inclination starts early. Even while puppies are still confined to their litters, they will routinely engage in play-fighting with their littermates, exploring their own physical capabilities and those of their friendly and usually willing adversaries. It's all a game at this stage, but in a real-life pack situation, the day would come soon enough when more assertive members of the group would begin to confront each other, vying for position in the pecking order of their extended family.

When two adult dogs square off in a contest of dominance, the competition isn't over until one of the two runs away, or in a more ritualistic display of submission, the weaker animal rolls over onto its back or side and willingly exposes its throat to the victor. The action communicates surrender—in fact, it's all that's usually needed to stop the advances of the winner.

Canine Communication

It might be surprising to learn that dogs have a rather sophisticated communication system, and they make full use of it. A cornerstone of this system is the animal's keen sense of smell, which, as we all know, is vastly superior to our own. The odor of urine, feces, anal sac excretions, as well as oil from the paws, cheeks, and chin all help a dog interact with its environment. The smell of these substances is as unique to each dog as fingerprints are to humans.

Urine markers: As might be expected of an animal that relies so much on its nose, scent marking plays an important role in this process. Urine marking, for example, is the method of choice in establishing territorial boundaries. A dominant dog that claims a certain territory will spray small amounts of urine on bushes, trees, fences, and buildings along the perimeter as a warning to intruders and passersby that this is its personal domain.

Of course, not all of the interlopers who read the warning will heed it, so your Doberman is obliged to patrol its territory regularly, adding fresh markings as it does so.

This leg-lifting behavior typically appears around five months of age, and the frequency of urination tends to follow a set pattern. Only a few drops are needed (males hardly ever empty their bladders completely, so there's always some to spare), and these are usually placed high up so they would be more immediately noticeable.

Urine marking also serves an important role in the reproductive process. Territorial markings by dominant male dogs are intended as much to advertise sexual readiness as they are for the maintenance of personal space.

Similarly, female dogs can also utilize specific urine markings to attract males. Pet owners with females will notice that they return to the same areas to smell whether males have urinated on their spots—not very romantic, but the system works.

It has been suggested that scent marking evolved as a kind of ritual that serves to familiarize and reassure an animal in a strange environment. That would explain why an otherwise house-trained dog will mark strategic areas of a new home.

Extremely fearful dogs may urinate uncontrollably in response to some real or imagined threat, just as highly submissive ones may urinate suddenly when we approach them, even if we are friendly and loving to them. Such dogs are suffering from lack of self-confidence, and their actions are a signal that they need more support and encouragement from us.

Note, however, that uncontrolled urination may also be a symptom of a urinary tract infection or other medical problem.

Anal markers: Fecal marking is a form of communication as well. It is less common than urine marking, but it can be used to claim territory in a much more demonstrative way.

A chance encounter between two male dogs usually follows a certain pattern. It, too, involves the sense of smell. Pausing briefly to size each other up from a distance, the dogs will approach each other gingerly, with head, ears, and tail held high. Circling around, each will sniff the other's hindquarters, where the anal sacs are found. Located on each side of the anus, the sacs are similar to, but much less pungent than, a skunk's scent glands. The material emitted from these sacs serves a communication function in that it is used by dogs to help identify each other. Anal sac excretions are also sprayed on objects to help demarcate territory.

Oil markers: Most people are unaware of the function of oil glands

Dogs see the world through their eyes, but they "read" about it with their noses.

mal is preparing to pounce. We cannot be sure how this behavior developed, but it is universal, which implies that it is inherited from the animal's ancestors.

Many aspects of dog behavior are related to the way of life of their long-forgotten predecessors. In stressful situations, for example, many dogs will seek a corner or hiding place where they will feel safe from possible "attack." Similar instincts may be at work with dogs that always want to sleep in a corner or with their backs to a wall.

It has also been suggested that when dogs make circling movements over the place they will sleep just before settling down, it too is a throwback to its primitive past, the action symbolizing the flattening of vegetation in the wild (for comfort as much as for unobstructed viewing). Another theory proposes that the animal is simply measuring the prevailing wind and positioning itself to best meet it.

Perhaps the most dramatic example of this genetic imprinting is the whole set of impulses and activities that surround parenting. The patterns of behavior that enable a bitch to care for her puppies certainly do not have to be learned—everything just "happens." Lack of interest in puppies after birth—the failure to clean them and warm them—is highly abnormal. As anyone who has ever stumbled upon a mother with newborns can attest, parents take more than a passing interest in their offspring.

on a dog's face and paws. When the animal stands in place and appears to be scraping at the ground with its paws, for example, it is actually rubbing oil onto the ground to mark the area. Facial oil can be used as a means of expression too, as some dogs rub their cheeks and chins on objects (and people) they claim as their own.

Genetic Imprinting

One of the side effects for dogs growing up in human company is that it may prolong juvenile behavior. To some extent, this is perhaps unavoidable, and in fact, most dog owners seem to appreciate and even encourage this behavior in their pets.

The invitation to play is easily identified: the dog drops its chest and forequarters to the ground, as if it is about to lay down, except that its rear legs remain standing, crouching slightly and leaning forward. The pose may be accompanied by barking and/or a repeated bobbing motion, as if the ani-

Behavior and Physical Health

Few pet owners suspect that their dog's behavior and emotional well-being are related to its physical health, but they are. There is strong evidence that behavioral problems can increase, if not actually cause, health problems in animals. Dogs that are self-destructive and display behavioral extremes are often susceptible to numerous ailments and diseases that rarely affect pets that are better balanced genetically and behaviorally. The most adaptable, self-confident dogs tend to have the fewest health problems.

Apparently, an animal's behavioral reaction to situations it encounters in life is mirrored by internal reactions within its body. Simply put, if a dog reacts confidently to external threats to its well-being, it also tends to be less susceptible to germ threats internally. Conversely, if a dog reacts to some perceived threat with extreme fear, its internal defense mechanisms—antibodies, white blood cells, and other components of its immune system—may be slow to respond when they are most needed. This temporary lapse in the body's defenses may be all that's needed for the onset of some illness that may otherwise have been avoided.

The Stress Factor

Stress is a primary source of health problems in pets, just as it is in humans. And while some people may think that a family dog leads a charmed and carefree life, stressful situations can arise at any time.

Since people and other animals are a major part of a pet's environment, negative changes in those relationships can indeed cause all kinds of behavior and health problems. Excessive fear, emotional frustration, or continuous confinement, for example, are almost guaranteed to manifest themselves in some demonstrative way.

Pets can develop "hot spots"—acute skin inflammations caused by biting at themselves, or lick granulomas— chronic infections caused by habitual licking, as well as other skin diseases as a result of inconsistent relationships with their owners. They are almost more prone to infections of the auditory, respiratory, gastrointestinal, genital, and urinary systems.

Animals need to maintain a balance of dominant and submissive behaviors, as one or the other may be appropriate in different situations. It is a great stress for a dominant animal to be confined or forced to submit all the time, just as it is stressful for a pet to receive inconsistent leadership from its owner. Both can be damaging.

Mating rituals—and pregnancy—can also be a great source of stress. Dominant dogs are more likely to get into fights during mating season; at the same time, because they tend to eat and sleep less and burn up more energy, they place a greater burden on their internal defenses.

Docile animals may not pursue sexual activity so voraciously, but they too, are subject to hormonal changes, and these can make them nervous and fearful. They often suffer a loss of appetite at this time, and they actually may appear to be ill.

Females display many physical and behavioral changes during mating season. Pregnancy, of course, is always stressful, but even during a safe and healthy one, females are bound to be more irritable, increasing the potential for abnormal behavior.

Interestingly, many pet behavior problems can be traced to changes in the mental dispositions of their owners. Sensitive to such things, dogs pick up on our mood and attitude changes, and sometimes they may be adversely affected by them, either because they may feel that perhaps they are somehow to blame, or that such negative feelings may be signaling a change in their status within the family.

Your Doberman must be shown that it is an accepted member of the family, with its own rightful share of food, territory, attention, and love. Overbearing or inconsistent leadership only serves to undermine this strategy.

Acknowledging submission.

Body Language

Declaring dominance: Body posture, facial expression, eye contact, and tail movement are important clues to a dog's state of mind. For example, an aggressive dog vying for dominance stares intently at other animals in its midst. Its head and ears are held high, the hair along its spine may bristle, and its tail will be held rigid in a straight line with its back. Its entire body appears stiff and tense. The dog will stare at its opponent with a fixed stare, at the same time circling it with a slow, cautious movement that is very different from the kind displayed during a casual encounter.

Declaring dominance.

Acknowledging submission: A submissive dog will react by turning its eyes and head downward or away from its tormentor's stare to acknowledge inferiority and avoid escalation of the conflict. Only two dogs of equally strong levels of confidence will maintain their stares until an actual fight erupts to determine ultimate superiority.

Readiness to attack: When a dog is about to attack, its mouth opens slightly and its muzzle wrinkles to expose its teeth. Snarls and growls accompany the reaction although some dogs attack silently—or from a distance, in which case, they tend to freeze momentarily, with the head held low and level with the back, the tail wagging slowly from side to side. Some dogs sink into a prone position before making their initial assault.

Dog fights vary in intensity, but they usually consist of more bravado than bloodshed. The most serious battles are likely to be those between dogs of the same sex, although a bitch not in season may feel compelled to drive off an unfamiliar male, snapping and growling at it with as much ferocity as it can muster, even though it's rare that any serious harm is intended. Interestingly, it is abnormal for a male dog to attack a female.

Have you noticed that puppies, too, are generally safe from the attack of adults, as if they understand that youngsters can't really be held responsible for their sometimes boisterous behavior? Some dogs, however, are less tolerant than others, and there are those that will bite a bothersome pup.

The Language of Sounds

You may never have given it much thought, but dogs really do speak to us. Barking, growling, whining, moaning, and other sounds make up what is actually a rather complex language system. Many dogs have little need to make sounds because their other communication signals are interpreted by us correctly, but the better we understand our Doberman, the quieter our home environment is likely to be.

Some dogs, especially fearful ones, can be quite vocal. If you carefully study the different sounds your pet makes, distinguishing subtle changes in sound quality and associating them with specific attitudes and behaviors, in time you may begin to have a pretty good idea of what your Doberman is trying to say to you.

Deeper, louder sounds indicate aggressiveness and dominance, while softer, higher-pitched sounds represent submissiveness. And believe it or not, this applies to humans as well. People who speak to dogs in an overly soft and sentimental voice are in effect assuming a submissive posture before the animal. This can send confusing signals to a dog that is supposed to be under our control.

All things considered, dogs don't display the wide range of

Readiness to attack.

emotions found in people, but an alert observer can indeed recognize feelings of happiness, sadness, anger, fear, confusion, curiosity, frustration, hopefulness and even love by picking up on the obvious—and not-so-obvious—clues in front of us.

When you learn to interpret a dog's behavior, you'll begin to sense what is a fairly complex animal communicating a wide variety of attitudes and desires.

History of the Breed

As the owner of a Doberman pinscher, it is important that you have at least a general awareness of the history of this noble breed. Certainly it is hoped that such knowledge will enhance your appreciation of your pet, but there is more to be gained than that. As the story behind the Doberman's development and its rise in popularity around the globe unfolds, you will better understand what a remarkable animal this dog really is and the proud tradition that it represents.

Early Developments

It is impossible to trace the exact evolutionary trail that brought us the Doberman pinscher; in the overall scheme of things, its ancestry is intertwined with that of all dogs, still a topic of considerable speculation. For our purposes, however, the Doberman's story begins in the early 1880s in the German province of Thuringia—specifically, the area around the town of Apolda—where a certain Herr Karl Louis Dobermann made his home.

A man of many responsibilities, Herr Dobermann served as the local tax and rent collector, a policeman and occasional night watchman, and as fate would have it, caretaker of the area's dog pound. In the course of his involvement with the many animals under his supervision, he gradually became obsessed with the idea of developing a special new breed of guard dog to protect him while he performed his various duties. He set out to do just that.

Unfortunately, although he made great advances with his breeding experiments and is fully credited with having "created" the breed we so admire today, Herr Dobermann was not in the habit of maintaining records of his work—a pity, for these would have proven to be a fascinating legacy today, both in scientific and

historical circles and among serious admirers of the breed. Of course, one really can't fault Herr Dobermann. Little did he know what far-reaching effects his humble experiments would have someday.

Nevertheless, it is widely accepted that the so-called German pinscher, an aggressive guard-type dog common in Germany at the time, provided the basis for his experiments. Many other breeds, though, played a role in the Doberman pinscher's evolution, most notably—and obviously—the Rottweiler, also the German shorthaired pointer, the weimaraner, the Manchester terrier, the Great Dane and perhaps even a few others.

All of these breeds contributed their best traits to Herr Dobermann's canine prototype—at least, that was the general idea—although the step-by-step development of the dog was really a matter of trial and error, as selective breeding always is to a great extent. As a matter of fact, some of the early breeding experiments had rather startling results by today's standards—such as the specimens said to have been born with long coats—but Herr Dobermann persisted and eventually prevailed. For those who have come to know and love the breed, that is legacy enough.

The result of Herr Dobermann's efforts was an alert, muscular, medium-size dog, black in color (initially at any rate) and fearless in disposition. The animals came to be known locally simply as "Dobermann's dogs," which indeed they were, but they were also called "Thuringian pinschers" (the former referring to its home province; the latter a German word meaning "terrier") and "Soldatenhunds" or "soldier dogs." From out of this mix came the name "Doberman pinscher," the second "n" in Dobermann having been dropped in many parts of the world. Except in the United States, the term "pinscher" was

*P*roperly trained, the Doberman is extremely devoted to its family and to children! However, any animal should be carefully supervised at all times when it is with youngsters.

later dropped because it was decided that the designation "terrier" was inappropriate for the breed.

The breed's evolution goes well beyond semantics, however, for the Doberman of today is considerably different than its early counterpart. For example, an initial breeding goal was a naturally bobbed tail rather than the docked version that is now preferred. It's also well known that early breeding attempts concentrated on developing the animal's aggressiveness, whereas the modern goal has become a no less physically capable dog, but one that is more even-tempered in nature.

Rise in Popularity

Herr Dobermann died in 1894, but by that time interest in the breed had taken hold in Germany, and other dedicated breeders were ready to take his place. One of these was Goswin Tischler, also of Apolda, whose von Groenland Kennels in 1895 produced Prinz Matzi von Groenland, the breed's first champion. Another resident of Apolda prominent in the breed's history is Otto Goeller, of von Thueringen Kennels, who is credited with establishing the first national "Dobermannpinscher Klub." That was in 1899, less than a year before the dog would gain official recognition in Germany by having its breed standards approved by the German Kennel Club. It was this certification procedure, in which Herr Goeller played a major role, that resulted in the official adoption of the breed's name. The "Dobermannpinscher" had arrived at a true measure of respectability.

A new dog breed doesn't come along every day, of course—especially such an impressive one as this—so the arrival of the Doberman caused considerable excitement, both among breeders and the public at large. Each year would see continuing leaps in the Doberman's popularity, as well as ongoing refinement in the dog's physi-

cal appearance. At the turn of the century, the black-and-tan variety received official acceptance, followed shortly by the brown and the blue, though the latter was slow to catch on. The same was true of the red Doberman, but it didn't arrive on the scene until many years later.

During the early 1900s, Dobermans began appearing in Switzerland, the Netherlands, France, Belgium, Italy, and Austria. In a few short years, they could be found as far east as Russia and as far west as the United States. The Doberman's future looked very bright indeed, and most likely it would have been were it not for World War I, which pretty much devastated its numbers in Europe. Thousands of Dobermans were recruited into military service, and those that were not had to contend with the same food shortage that gripped the human population.

As a consequence of these conditions, many Doberman breeders who could not bear the thought of seeing their animals' lives wasted in war sold their stock, including some of their finest specimens, to dog fanciers in other parts of the world, especially the United States. Germany's loss was the world's gain, however, for it inadvertently spurred the breed's climb to international prominence.

The breed in Germany began to recover somewhat after the war, but foreign sales continued as Doberman registrations—in North America as well as Europe—kept growing. World War II would virtually bring an end to exportation, but by that time the breed was on firm footing in many countries.

Today, the Doberman pinscher (or "Dobermann") is found on every continent, as are the many specialty clubs that continue to advance the breed. None, however, is more active than the Doberman Pinscher Club of America, founded in 1921. Largely through the efforts of its members, the

Doberman now ranks near the top of all registrations in this country.

Arrival in America

The first Doberman to be registered in the United States was named Doberman Intelectus, owned by Carl Schulyheiss. That was back in 1908, the same year that Theodore Yaeger, of Rochester, New York, opened his Doberman Kennels, which eventually produced Doberman Dix, the first American-bred Doberman to attain a championship in this country.

More firsts followed over the course of the years. In 1924, Burga von Kumpmuehl became the first blue Doberman to attain a championship; in 1926, Carlo of Rhinegold, bred by world-famous Doberman authority Francis F. H. Fleitman, of Westphalia Kennels, became the first American-bred winner of a Best in Show title; finally, in 1939, a dog by the name of Sieger Ferry von Rauhfelsen, owned by Mrs. Hartley Dodge of Giralda Farms, became the first to win the Best in Show title at the Westminster Kennel Club Dog Show, today as then the premiere dog event in this country.

Military Service

The Doberman, as we have learned, was specifically bred and developed to be a guard dog, and so it was infused with traits that would help it excel in this role—alertness, fearlessness, strength, and agility. These very same qualities, together with its strong sense of loyalty and its ability to learn quickly, made it ideal for both police and military work as well. Dogs of all kinds have been accompanying soldiers—both as guards and attack animals—for centuries. The Doberman was a latecomer to these ranks, but its performance to date has been nothing less than spectacular. No wonder the breed has become such a popular choice among armies and police forces all over the world.

By the start of World War I, the Germans had several thousand dogs—including Dobermans and German shepherds—trained for guard and rescue duty. The British, too, had successfully instructed dogs to work in similar capacities. The animals performed bravely and well, as their handlers and trainers had always said they would, but their use was still somewhat limited at that time.

Real strides in the art of canine warfare came during World War II, when dogs—the Doberman prominent among them—were used in great numbers, and in a great many ways, by both sides. It is estimated that the U.S. Armed Forces (Army, Navy, Marines) commissioned at least 250,000 dogs during the war years! (The Marines later adopted the Doberman as its official mascot.) And at that time, just about every army in Europe had dog soldiers of its own.

War dogs were trained to do all kinds of work—tracking, scouting, sentry and patrol duty, locating wounded in the field, locating enemy positions (also snipers, supply caches and so forth), detecting mines and other booby traps, physically assaulting and subduing the enemy, and guarding prisoners. Russian and German troops were even known to use them as anti-tank weapons. With a load of explosives strapped to their bodies, the dogs were trained to make their way underneath enemy tanks, at which time a remote-controlled detonator would be activated, killing the occupants, and the dogs too, of course.

Though some dogs seemed to come pretty close, none (not even a Doberman) excelled in every area of performance, nor were any expected to. Typically, a dog was assigned to a specific field of training following a preliminary evaluation, after which its future was determined by a combination of its own performance and its trainer's best judgment.

Training for the Public Sector

For both police and military purposes, dogs are initially selected on the basis of several criteria, one of the first of which is age. Specific requirements may vary, but five years is usually the limit. Minimum height and weight requirements (which any normal Doberman can meet) must also be satisfied, and of course the animal must be in good health. After that comes an assessment of learning ability—another prime consideration, certainly, for animals whose duties could be critical to the well-being of the people around them. By that same token, it wouldn't do for a dog to be gun-shy. Finally, dogs have to exhibit a certain level of aggressiveness in their behavior—not to the point of outright savagery, but a certain amount of brazenness is nevertheless desirable. On the other hand, dogs that are lethargic and take no interest in strangers, or that are easily approached and coaxed into tail-

These Dobermans have been trained to be responsive household pets.

wagging and friendship—indeed the kind that most of us might like to have as a pet—must be summarily dismissed.

Today, training and use of dogs in military and in law enforcement capacities overlap in many areas. Dogs in either group may become involved in patrol work, crowd control, sniffing out narcotics or explosives, tracking, and, if and when the situation calls for it, the subjugation of a human adversary. Dobermans have been used successfully in all of these areas, and their reputation as a group is second to none.

Training for the Private Sector

In the private sector, Dobermans have been worked in just about every capacity imaginable—though their use as guard dogs continues to head the list. They have also been used effectively as hunting dogs, for example, even though they are not the hunting dog of choice for most sportsmen. Nevertheless, the Doberman's nose is as keen as any dog's, and the animal can indeed be trained to retrieve, to track, and even to "go on point."

The Official German Standard

The first breed standard for the Doberman pinscher dates back to 1899, only a few short years after the breed had been developed. Drawn up by the then fledgling National Doberman Pinscher Club of Germany, the standard was eventually adopted by all countries recognizing the breed, including the United States, which officially acknowledged the Doberman in 1908.

A breed standard attempts to define, primarily (but not exclusively) in physical terms, what are considered to be the ideal attributes of a particular breed of dog. Thus, the standard represents a list of criteria by which purebred dogs may be compared and evaluated for excellence. Of utmost importance to dog owners who compete in show circles and to breeders whose reputation and livelihood depend on the measurable quality of their stock, it should likewise not escape the attention of dog owners who intend to breed their pets on even a limited basis, or owners who simply seek the assurance that their animals exemplify the true essence of the breed that they represent.

A departure from the breed standard is known as a "fault," and while a dog in the show ring will be penalized for any such deviation from the norm, however minor, it must be distinguished from what is known as a "disqualifying fault," the latter being so prominent that it is beyond acceptable limits of conformation.

As is still characteristic of the breed today, the German Standard required that dogs be muscular and powerfully built, but not to the point of being overly massive. Rather, a certain look of nimbleness, of restrained energy waiting to be unleashed, was the sought after ideal in general physical appearance, this being a true reflection of its intense and vigorous temperament.

In terms of specifics, the German Standard allowed a shoulder height that ranged form 21.6 to 25.6 inches (55–65 cm) for males, 18.9 to 21.6 inches (48–55 cm) for females. Overall body length, measured from the lower back of the skull to the first tail joint, averaged 27.5 inches (70 cm), with the tail cropped to a length not exceeding 5.9 inches (15 cm).

Then, as now, much attention was placed on the appearance of the animal's head. The top of the skull could be flat or slightly arched, but always broadening at the forehead and extending downward to the muzzle. Measuring from the back of the skull to the tip of the nose, the acceptable length of the head was 10 inches, or no more than a fraction less. Cheeks, in turn, had to be flat and muscular,

with lips clinging tightly to the powerful jaws, and the well-developed teeth had to close in perfect alignment. Medium-sized eyes, which could only be dark brown in the early days of the breed's history, had to convey an expression of intelligence and alertness, at the same time exhibiting a certain trace of gentleness that was perhaps a bit misleading, considering the breed's aggressive nature. Finally, ears had to be cropped, but not to the extent that they appeared short or overly pointy.

When the Doberman first appeared, it was common practice to crop almost all of the ear on working dogs, the theory being that, under adverse conditions, it left precious little for a foe—be it man or beast—to latch onto. Only later did the long triangular crop come into vogue in some parts of the world, and this is a cosmetic alteration more than anything else, precisely why it is forbidden in many countries, including Britain and Australia. Say what you will about the merits of this practice, it's hard to deny that a Doberman so transformed isn't more regal looking.

Although the original German Standard laid a solid foundation for the breed's rise to prominence, it apparently did not accommodate every last concern of Doberman fanciers, nor did it take into account certain physiological changes that were simply the result of the breed's ongoing evolution. It was precisely for these reasons that the Doberman Pinscher Club or America (with the approval of the American Kennel Club has opted to amend the German Standard—several times—over the years.

The organization's membership was also concerned that a lack of direction, of clearly defined goals and limits, might ultimately encourage breeders to concentrate on certain traits at the expense of others, perhaps forever altering the breed in the process.

1. skull; 2. ears;
3. stop; 4. cheek;
5. muzzle; 6. shoul-
der, 7. chest; 8. rib
cage; 9. forequar-
ters; 10. front
pastern; 11. rib
cage; 12. stifle;
13. hindquarters;
14. hock; 15. rear
pastern; 16. loin;
17. tail; 18. withers;
19. neckline

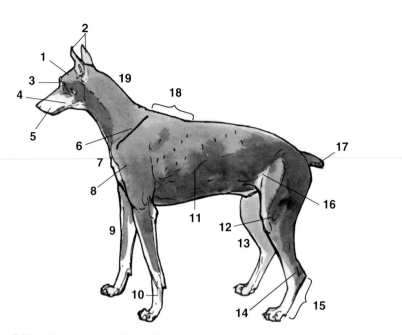

The Official American Standard

Action was first taken in 1935, when the American club secured approval for what became the new American Standard for the breed. Its primary departure concerned adjustments in height and head size. A 1948 revision did likewise, but also more clearly spelled out the animal's preferred disposition, which was that it be aggressive and fearless, but never vicious; nor could the dog be timid, this being equally undesirable. Yet another revision, approved in 1969, demanded a proper tooth count whereby more than three missing teeth was deemed a disqualifying fault; it also officially acknowledged the Isabella, or fawn-colored, Doberman.

The current American Standard was approved by the AKC in 1982 and reformatted in 1992.

General Appearance

The appearance is that of a dog of medium size, with a body that is square. Compactly built, muscular and powerful, for great endurance and speed. Elegant in appearance, of proud carriage, reflecting great nobility and temperament. Energetic, watchful, determined, alert, fearless, loyal, and obedient.

Height

At the withers: Dogs, 26 to 28 inches (ideal, about 27½ inches); Bitches, 24 to 26 inches (ideal, about 25½ inches). The height, measured vertically from the ground to the highest point of the withers, equalling the length measured from the forechest to the rear projection of the upper thigh. Length of head, neck, and legs in proportion to length and depth of body.

Head

Long and dry, resembling a blunt wedge in both frontal and profile views. When seen from the front, the head widens gradually toward the base of the ears in a practically unbroken line.

Eyes: Almond-shaped, moderately deep set, with vigorous, energetic expressions. Iris of uniform color, ranging from medium to darkest brown in black dogs; in reds, blues, and fawns, the color of the iris blends with that of the markings, the darkest shade being preferable in every case.

Ears: Normally cropped and carried erect. The upper attachment of the ear, when held erect, is on a level with the top of the skull.

Skull: Top of skull flat, turning with slight stop to bridge of muzzle, with muzzle line extending parallel to top line of skull. Cheeks flat and muscular. Lips lying close to jaws. Jaws full and powerful, well filled under the eyes.

Teeth: Strongly developed and white. Lower incisors upright and touching inside of upper incisors—a true scissors bite. Forty-two *correctly placed teeth*, 22 in the lower, 20 in the upper jaw. Distemper teeth shall not be penalized. *Disqualifying Faults:* overshot of more than ³⁄₁₆ of an inch; undershot of more than ⅛ of an inch; four or more missing teeth.

Nose: Solid black on black dogs, dark brown on red ones, dark gray on blue ones, dark tan on fawns.

Neck: Proudly carried, well muscled and dry. Well arched, with nape of neck widening gradually toward body. Length of neck proportioned to body and head.

Neck, Topline, Body

Withers: pronounced and forming the highest point of the body. Back short, firm, of sufficient width, and muscular at the loins, extending in a straight line from withers to the slightly rounded croup.

Brisket: reaching deep to the elbow.

Chest: broad, with forechest well defined.

Ribs: well sprung from the spine, but flattened in lower end to permit elbow clearance.

Belly: well tucked up, extending in a curved line from the brisket.

Loins: wide and muscled.

Hips: broad and in proportion to the body, breadth of hips being approximately equal to breadth of body at rib cage and shoulders.

Tail: Docked at approximately second joint, appears to be a continuation of the spine, and is carried only slightly above the horizontal when the dog is alert.

Forequarters

Shoulder blade: sloping forward and downward at a 45-degree angle to the ground, meets the upper arm at an angle of 90 degrees. Length of shoulder blade and upper arm are equal. Height from elbow to withers approximately equals height from ground to elbow.

Legs: seen from front and side, perfectly straight and parallel to each other from elbow to pastern; muscled and sinewy, with heavy bone. In normal pose and when gaiting, the elbows lie close to the brisket.

Pasterns: firm and almost perpendicular to the ground. Dewclaws may be removed.

Feet: well arched, compact, and catlike, turning neither in nor out.

Hindquarters

The angulation of the hindquarters balances that of the forequarters.

Hip Bone: falls away from the spinal column at an angle of about 30 degrees, producing a slightly rounded, well filled out croup.

Upper shanks: at right angles to the hip bones, are long, wide, and well muscled on both sides of thigh, with clearly defined stifles. Upper and lower shanks are of equal length. While the dog is at rest, hock to heel is perpendicular to the ground. Viewed from the rear, the legs are straight, parallel to each other, and wide enough apart to fit in with a properly built body. Dewclaws, if any, are generally removed.

Cat Feet: as on front legs, turning neither in nor out.

Coat
Smooth-haired, short, hard, thick, and close-lying. Invisible gray undercoat on neck permissible.

Doberman pups may look somewhat pathetic with their ears taped up after cropping. This purely cosmetic alteration is a short-lived inconvenience that they will quickly forget.

Color, and Markings
Allowed Colors: Black, red, blue, and fawn (Isabella). *Markings:* Rust, sharply defined, appearing above each eye and on muzzle, throat and forechest, on all legs and feet, and below tail. White patch on chest, not exceeding ½ square inch, permissible. *Disqualifying Fault:* Dogs not of an allowed color.

Gait
Free, balanced, and vigorous, with good reach in the forequarters and good driving power in the hindquarters. When trotting, there is a strong rear-action drive. Each rear leg moves in line with the foreleg on the same side. Rear and front legs are thrown neither in nor out. Back remains strong and firm. When moving at a fast trot, a properly built dog will single track.

Temperament
Energetic, watchful, determined, alert, fearless, loyal, and obedient. *The judge shall dismiss from the ring any shy or vicious Doberman.*

Shyness: A dog shall be judged fundamentally shy if, refusing to stand for examination, it shrinks away from the judge; if it fears approach from the rear; if it shies at sudden and unusual noises to a marked degree.

Viciousness: A dog that attacks or attempts to attack either the judge or its handler is definitely vicious. An aggressive or belligerent attitude toward other dogs shall not be deemed viciousness.

Faults:
The foregoing description is that of the ideal Doberman pinscher (as defined by the Doberman Pinscher Club of America). Any deviation from the above described dog must be penalized to the extent of the deviation.

The Official British Standard
Another breed standard worth noting here is the British one, drawn up by the Kennel Club of that country. While similar to the American Standard in most respects, the British Standard differs in several key areas.

The most prominent departure, aside from the ban on ear-cropping, is the fact that the breed in England is simply known as the Dobermann (with two n's and without the "pinscher" designation).

The British Standard also states that white markings on the dog's coat "are highly undesirable," whereas in the American version, a white patch on the chest is acceptable, provided that it does not exceed ½ square inch. Another difference is the British requirement that *all* dewclaws be removed. While the American Standard does indeed insist that rear dewclaws be sacrificed, it leaves the option open on the front feet, commenting only that they "may" be removed. Finally, there is a slight discrepancy in the rules governing tail-cropping. The American Standard requires that it be done "at approximately the second joint"; its British counterpart offers the option of doing so "at the first or second joint."

Despite the differences, both countries can rightly take credit for promoting and maintaining the highest standards of excellence—standards that continue to keep the Doberman in the forefront of breeds in its class.

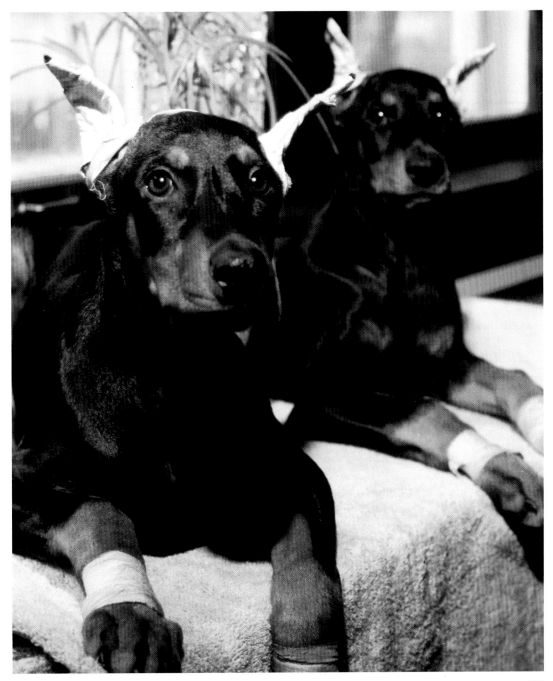

Useful Literature and Addresses

Addresses

Doberman Pinscher Club of
America (DPCA)*
Mrs. Tommie F. Jones,
　Corresponding Secretary
　4840 Thomasville Road
　Tallahassee, Florida 32308

American Kennel Club
　51 Madison Avenue
　New York, NY 10038

Australian National Kennel Club
　Royal Show Grounds
　Ascot Vale,
　Victoria, Australia

Canadian Kennel Club
　111 Eglington Avenue
　Toronto 12,
　Ontario, Canada

Irish Kennel Club
　41 Harcourt Street
　Dublin 2, Ireland

The Kennel Club
　1-4 Clargis Street
　Picadilly
　London, W7Y 8AB, England

New Zealand Kennel Club
　P.O. Box 523
　Wellington, New Zealand

Books

In addition to the most recent
edition of the official publication of
the AKC, *The Complete Dog
Book*, published by Howell Book
House, Inc., in New York, the following publications contain useful
information.

Alderton, David. *The Dog Care
Manual.* Hauppauge, New
York: Barron's Educational
Series, Inc., 1986.

Baer, Ted. *Communicating With
Your Dog.* Hauppauge, New
York: Barron's Educational
Series, Inc., 1989.

——. *How To Teach Your Old
Dog New Tricks.* Hauppauge,
New York: Barron's
Educational Series, Inc., 1991.

Frye, Fredric L. *First Aid for Your
Dog.* Hauppauge, New York:
Barron's Educational Series,
Inc., 1987.

Klever, Ulrich. *The Complete
Book of Dog Care.* Hauppauge,
New York: Barron's
Educational Series, Inc., 1989.

Lorenz, Konrad. *Man Meets Dog.*
London and New York:
Penguin Books, 1967.

Pinney, Christopher. *Guide to
Home Pet Grooming.*
Hauppauge, New York: Barron's
Educational Series, Inc., 1990.

Smythe, Reginald H. *The Mind of
the Dog.* London: Thomas,
Bannerstone House, 1961.

Ullman, Hans–J., and Evamaria
Ullman. *The New Dog
Handbook.* Hauppauge, New
York: Barron's Educational
Series, Inc., 1985.

country.

* This address may change as new
officers are elected. This latest list-
ing can always be obtained from
the American Kennel Club.

Index